I0486586

© MOTLEY MAGAZINE
&
© WORM LITERATURE MMXXIII

motley   mag
volume   3
(issue   3)

First edition: February, 2023

Cover design: João Bresler
Model: Marcel Gago

© All rights reserved
Printed somewhere on Earth i hope
ISBN: 978-1-4478-8381-4.

Worm Literature
MMXXIII

Motley Mag
VOL.3

houghts and visuals
elected

Editors And Collaborators Of The MOTLEY MAGAZINE:

EDITOR. João Bresler @*oysterboiwho*

COLLABORATORS.
(in order of appearance, with the first piece being the guide in case of having contributed with multiple pieces)

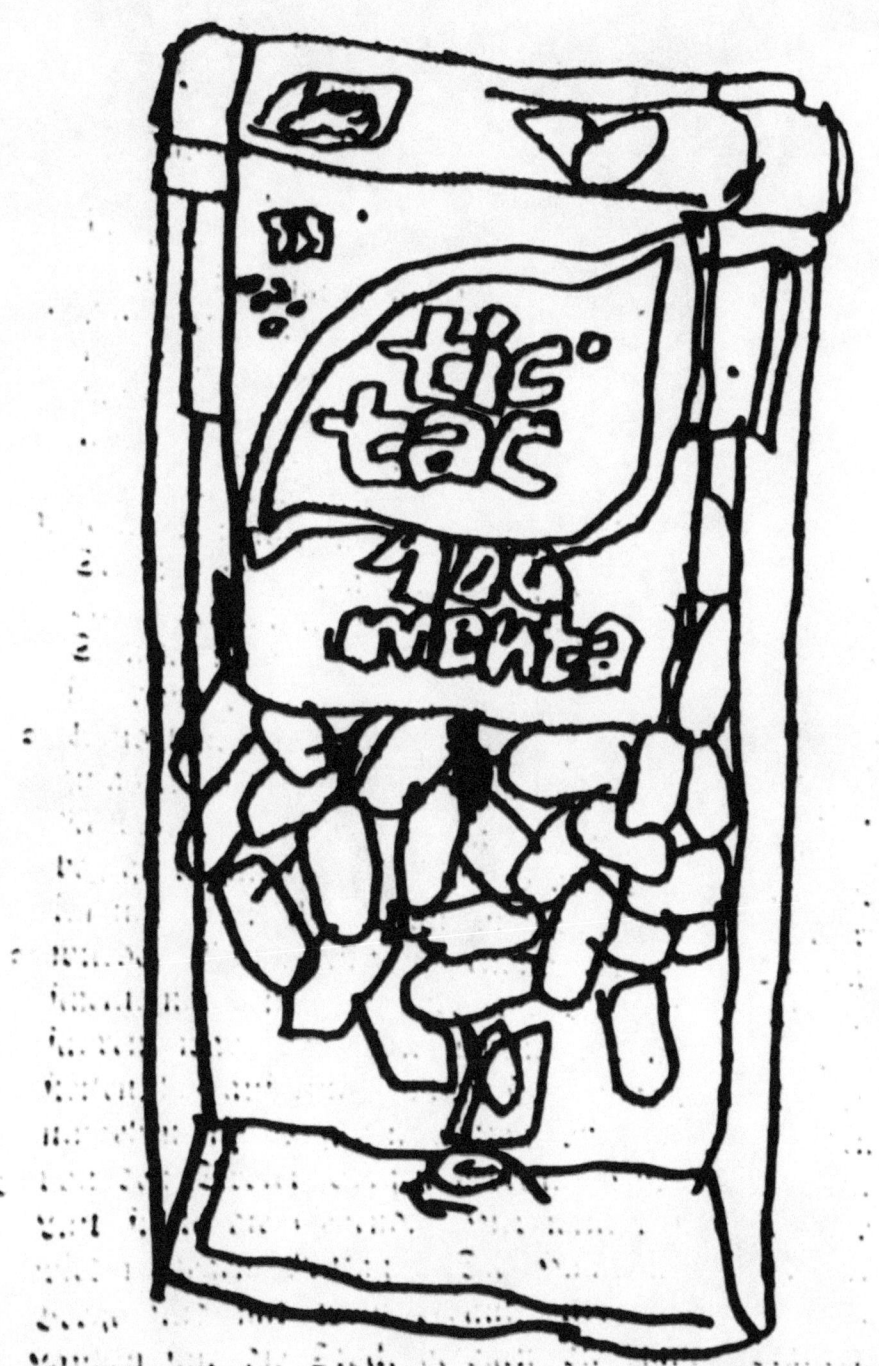

3

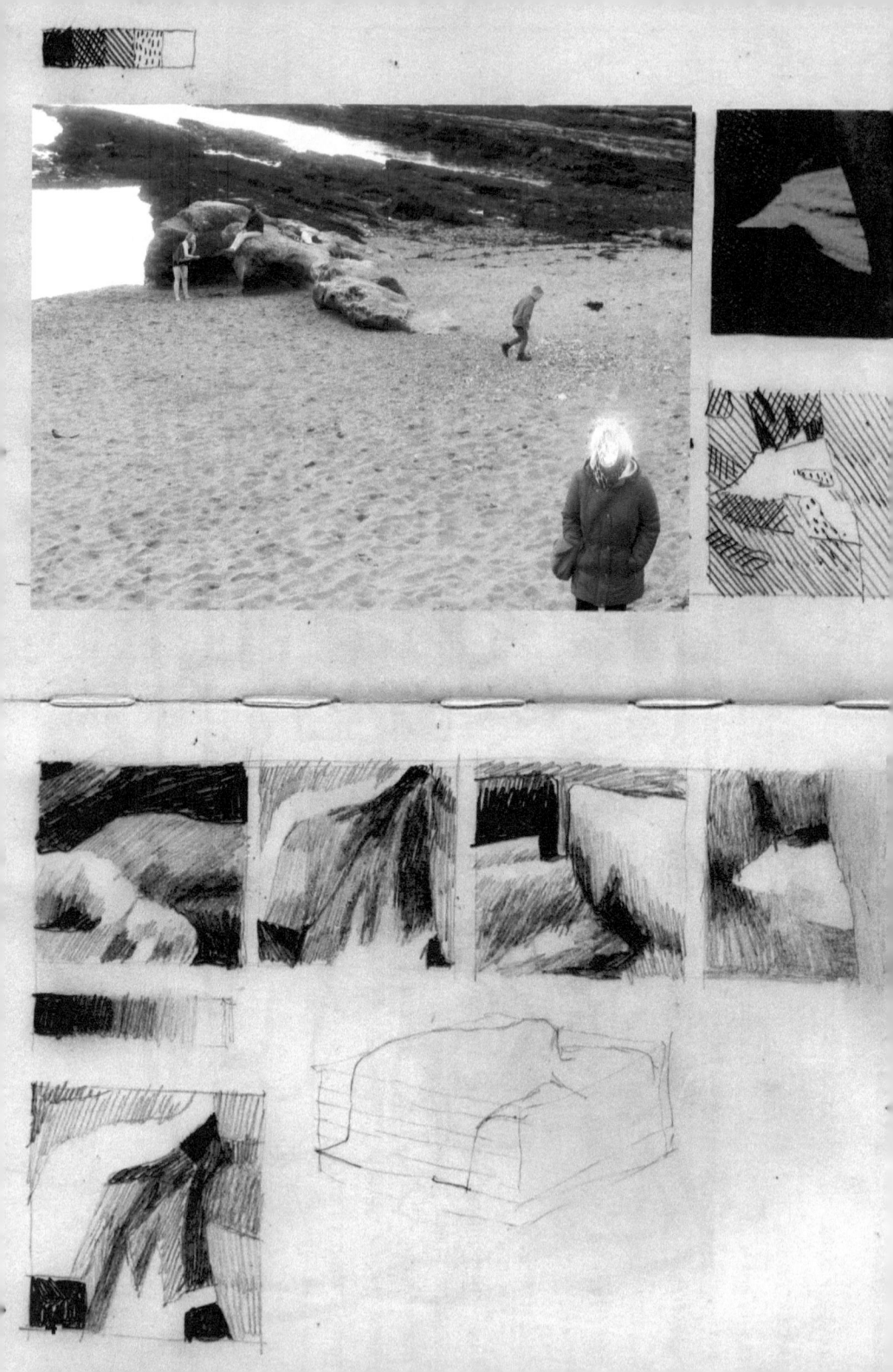

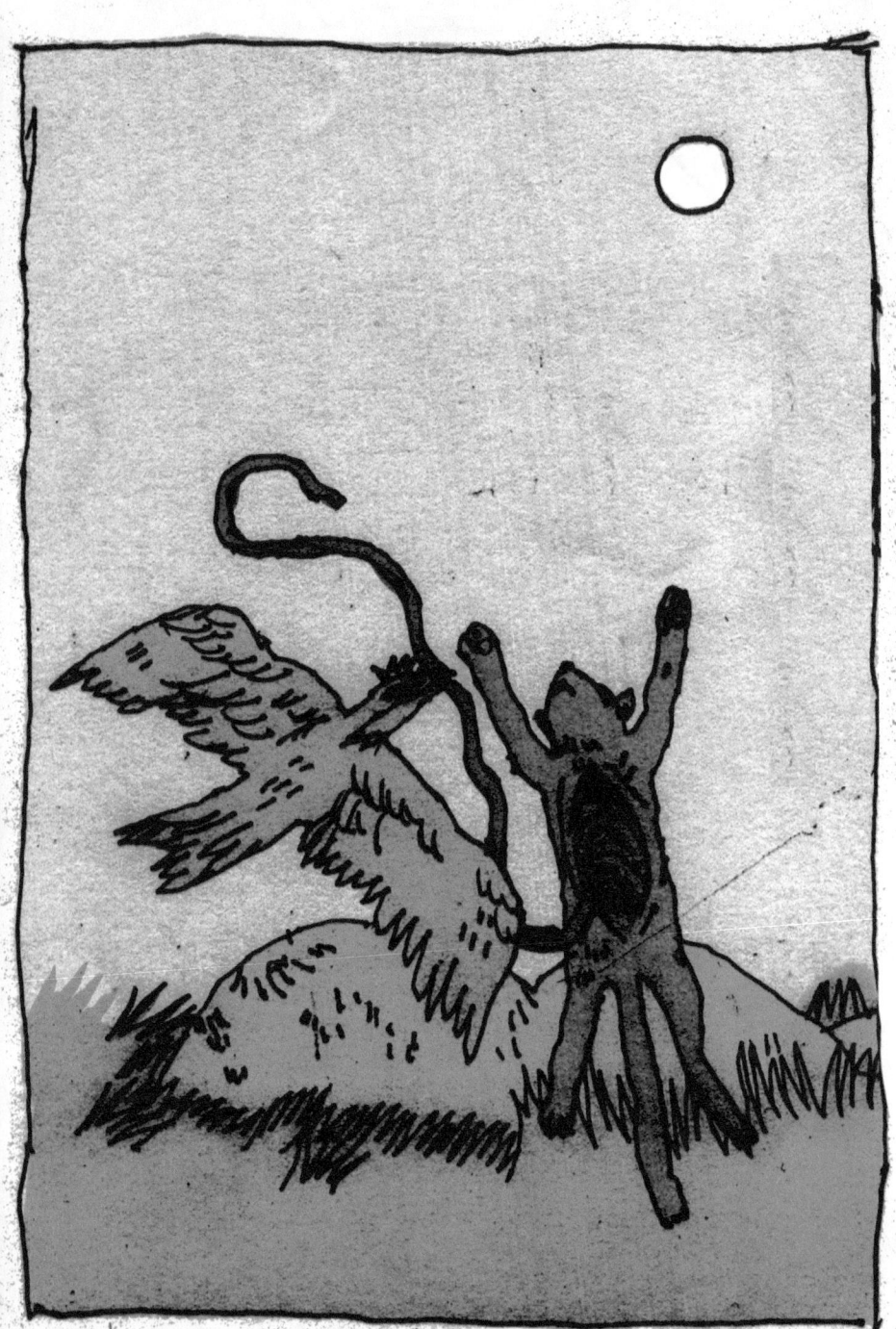

5

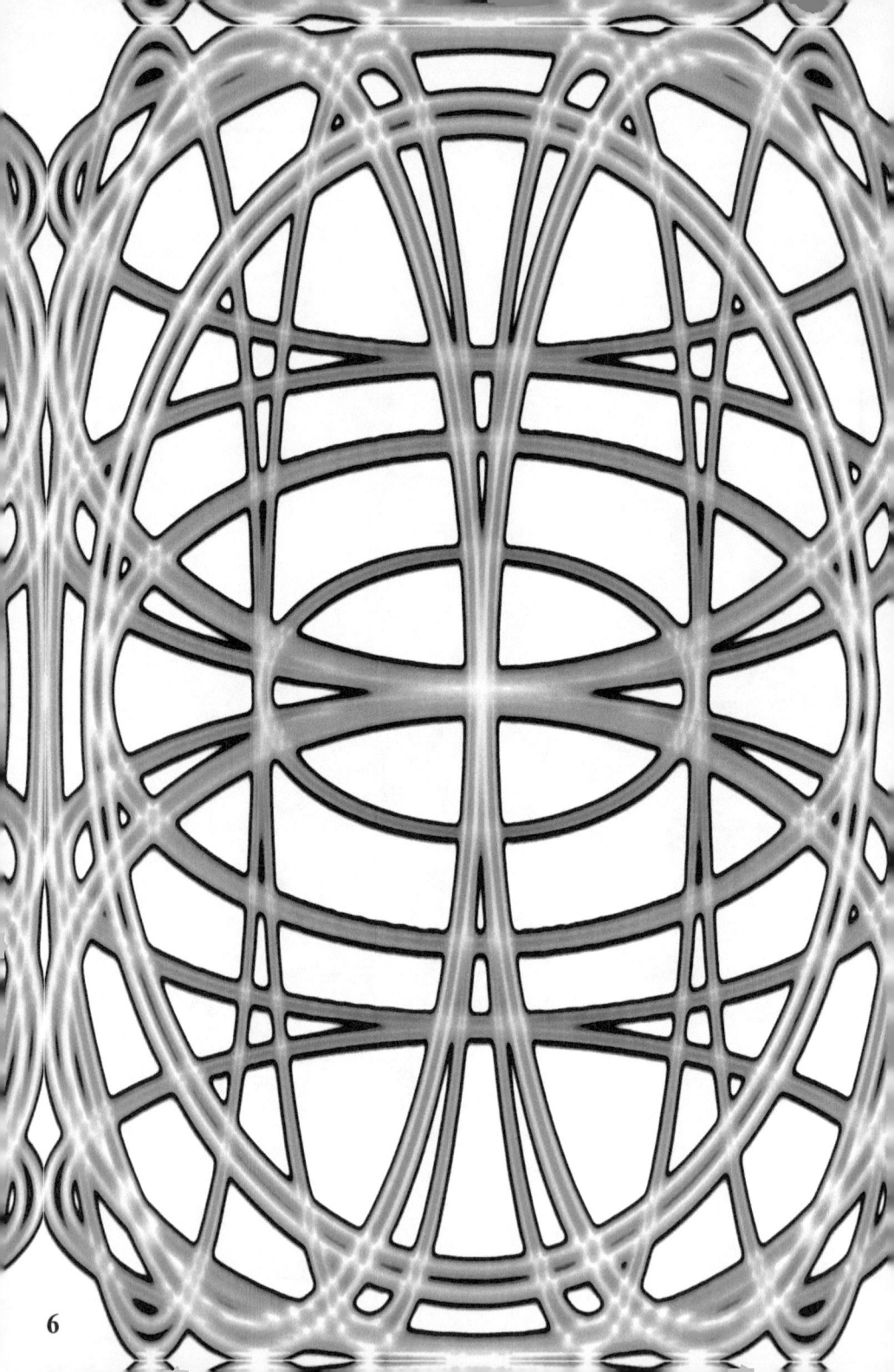

6

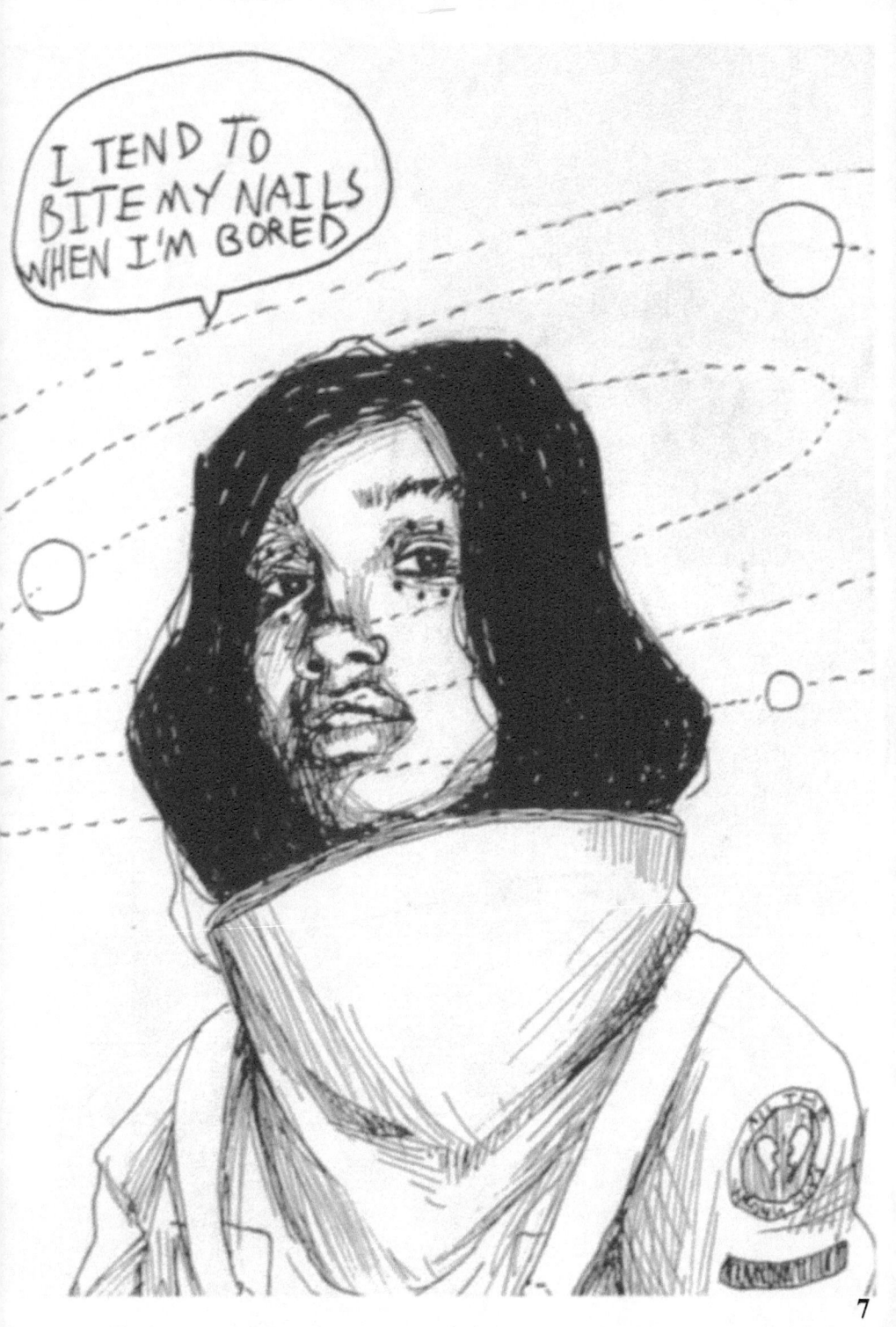

7

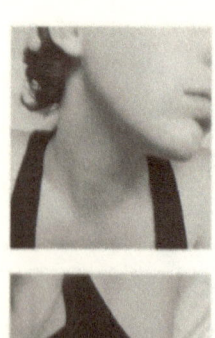
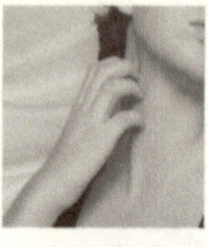
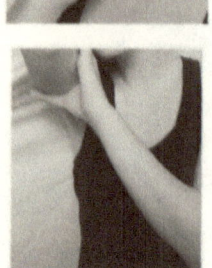
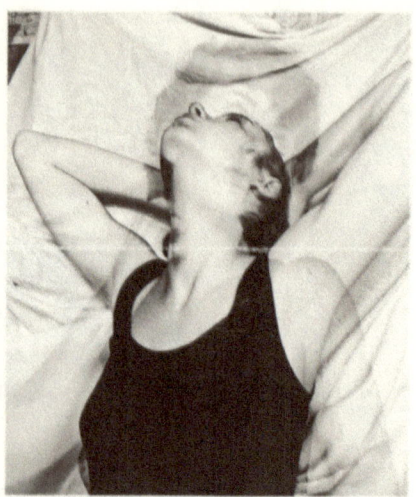
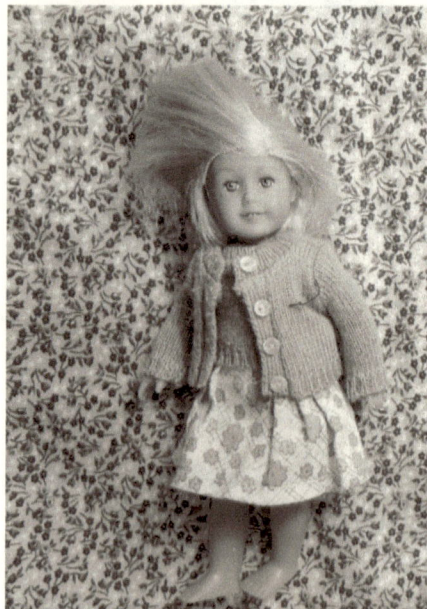

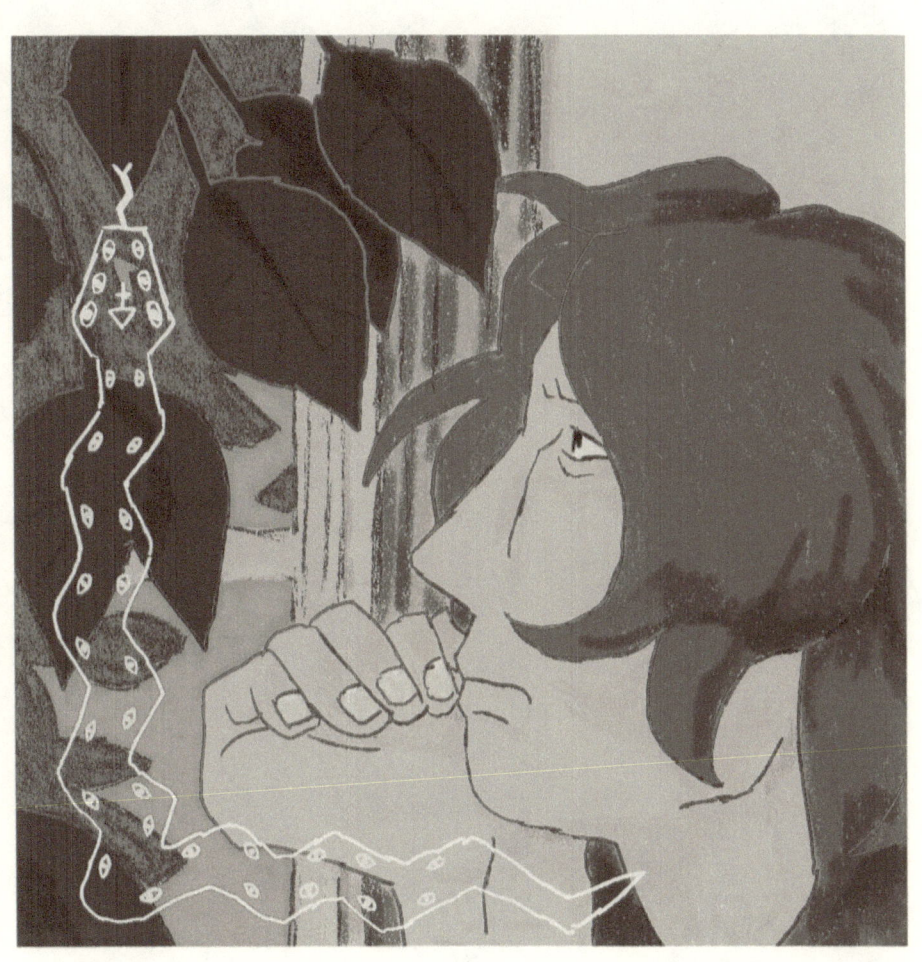

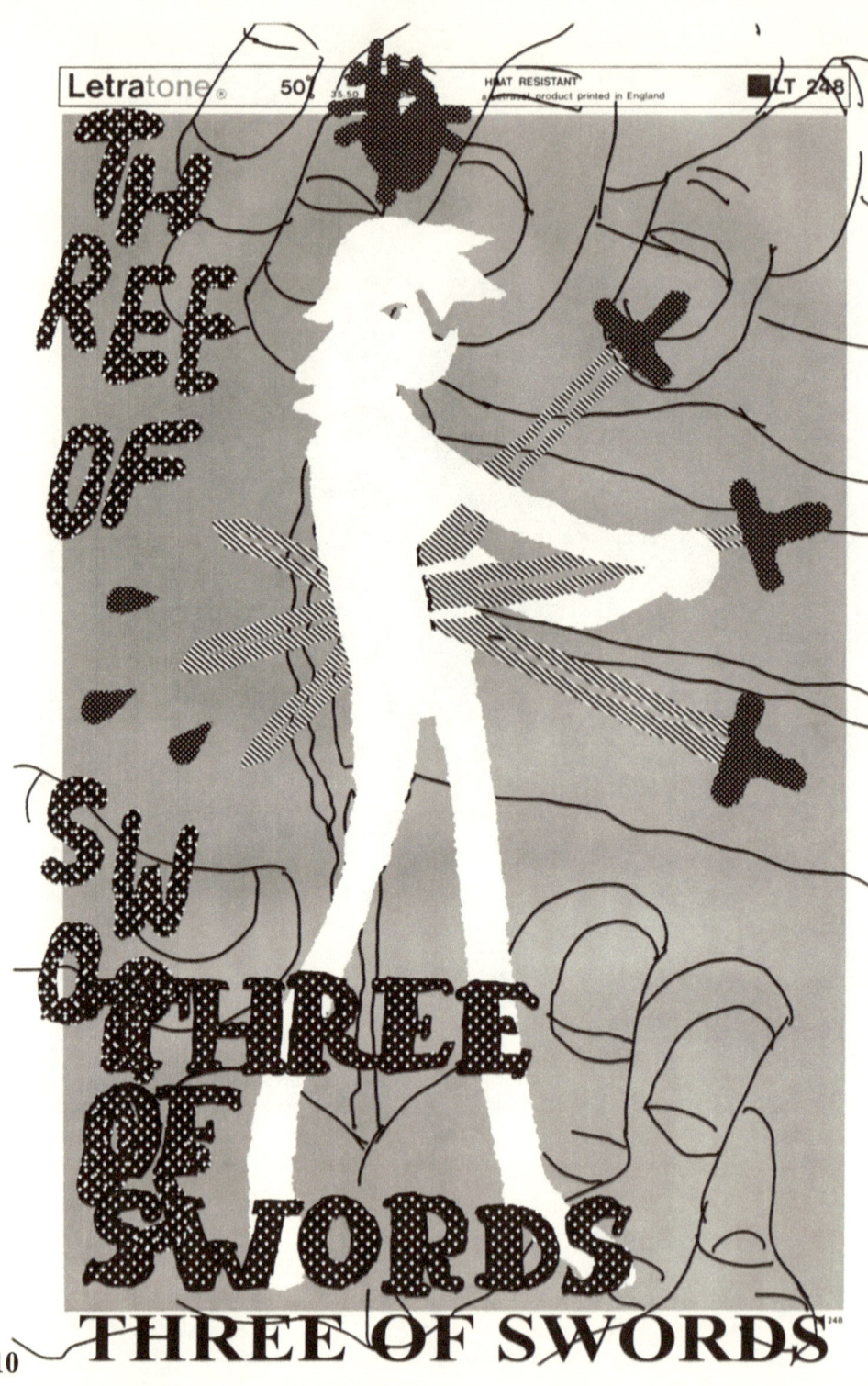

THREE OF SWORDS

THREE OF SWORDS

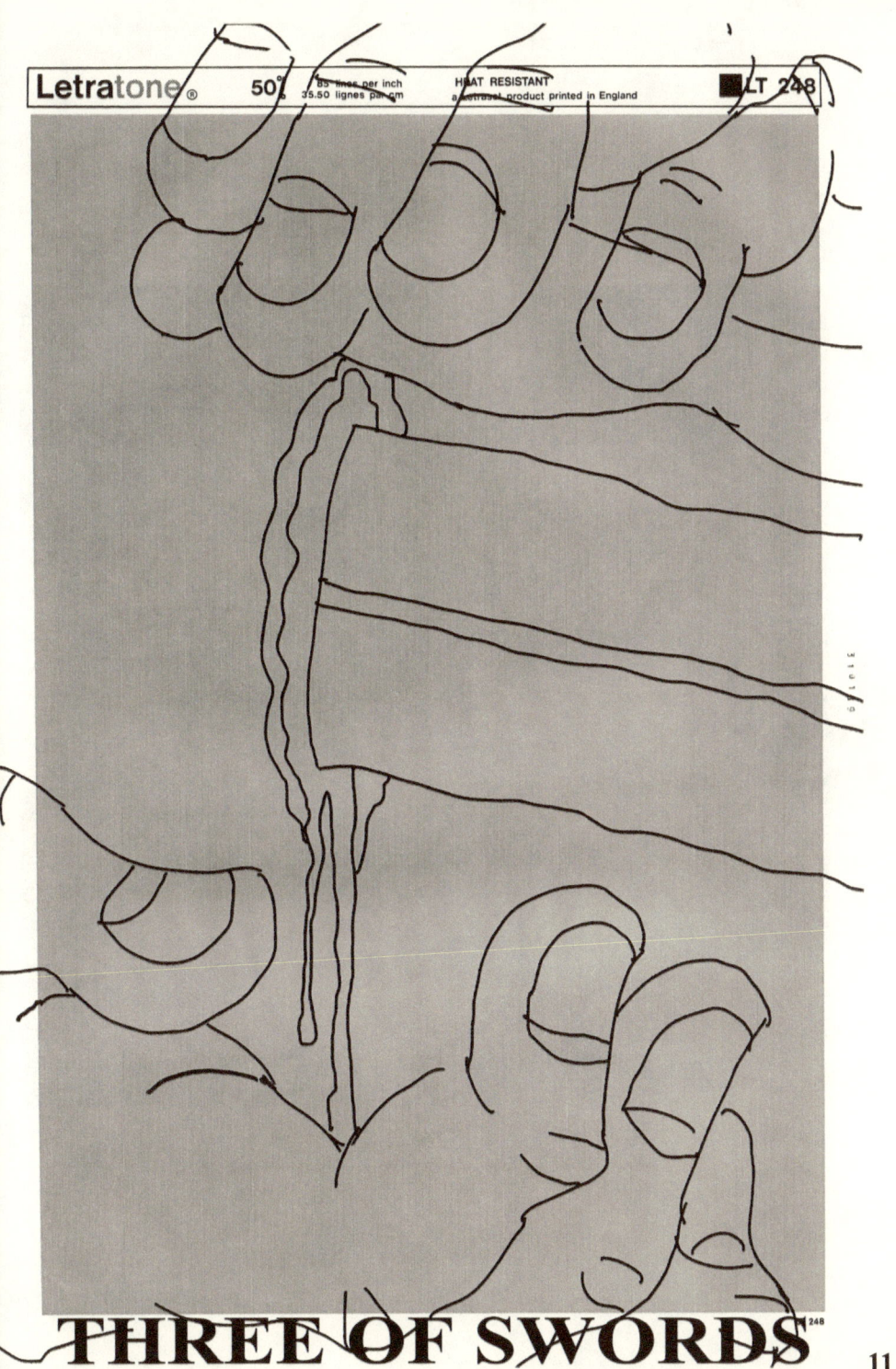

Letratone® 50% 85 lines per inch / 35.50 lignes par cm   HEAT RESISTANT / a letraset product printed in England   LT 248

THREE OF SWORDS

11

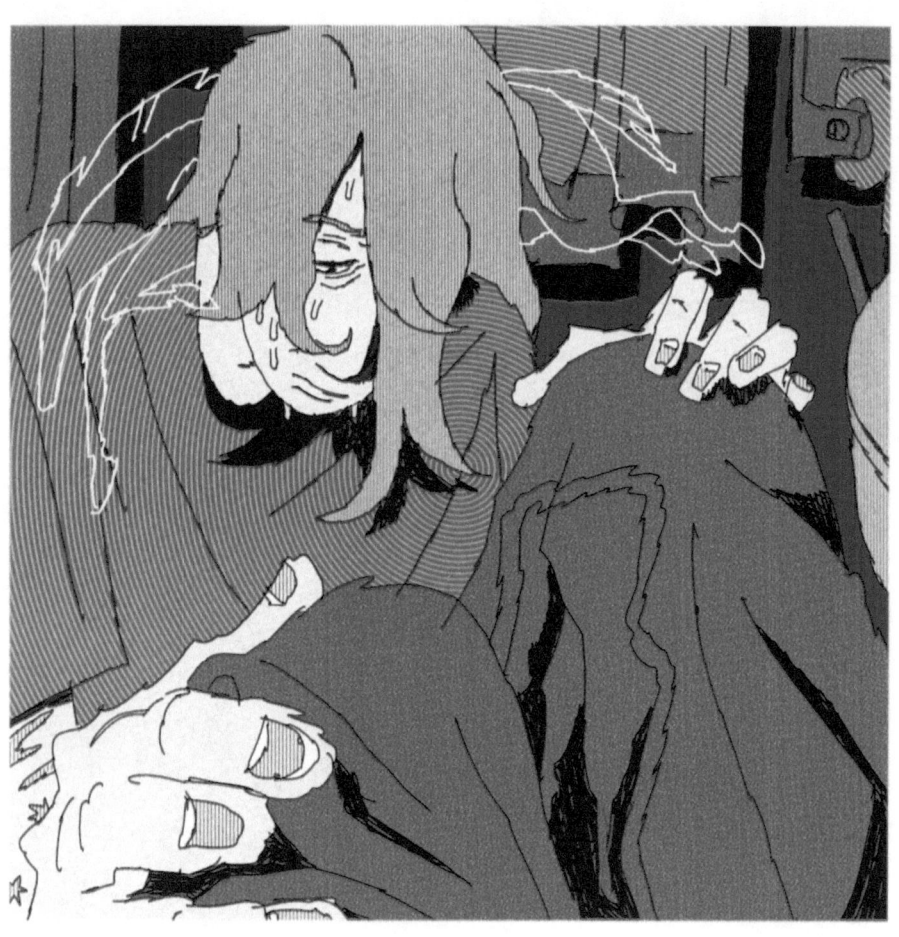

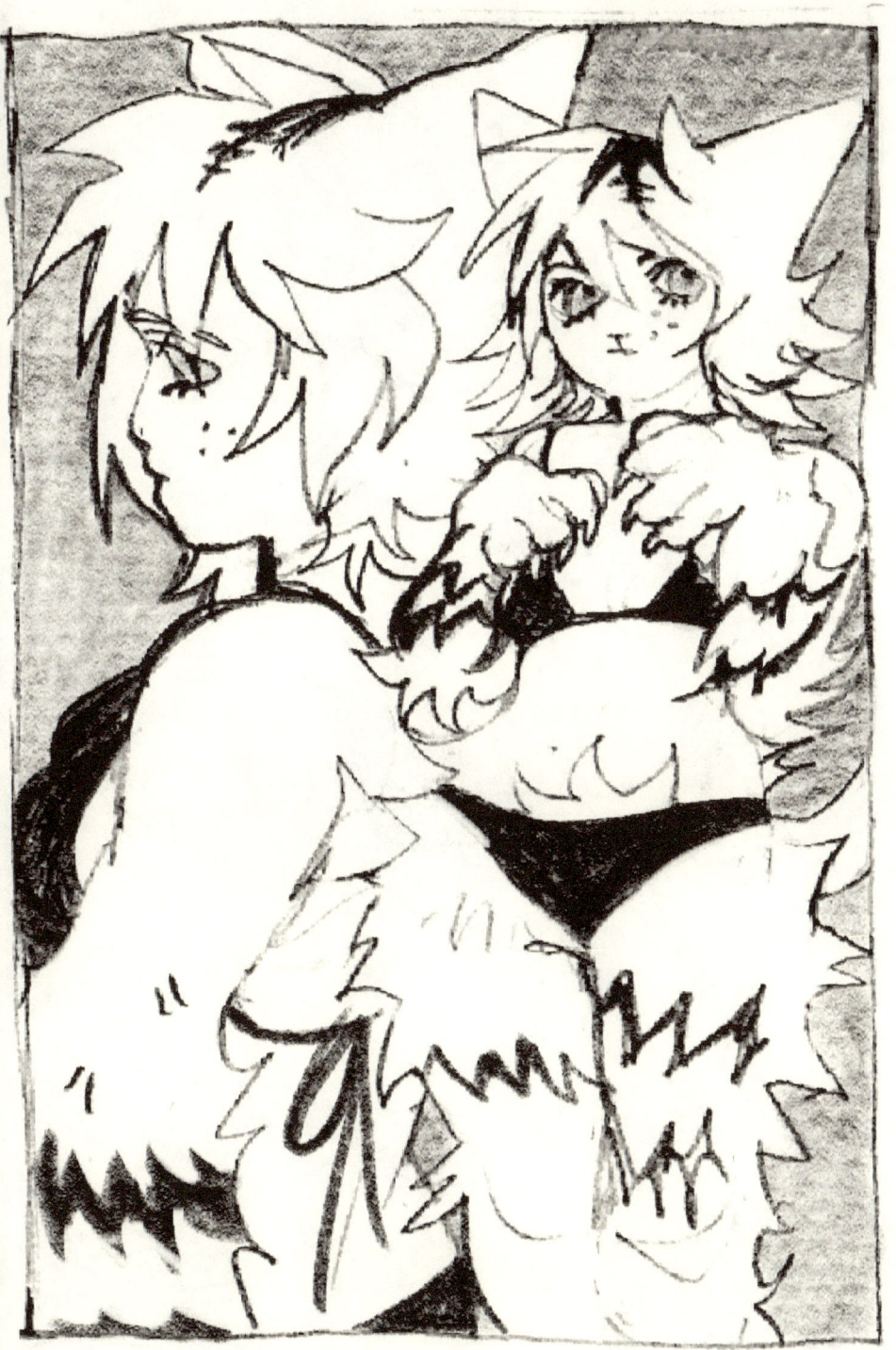

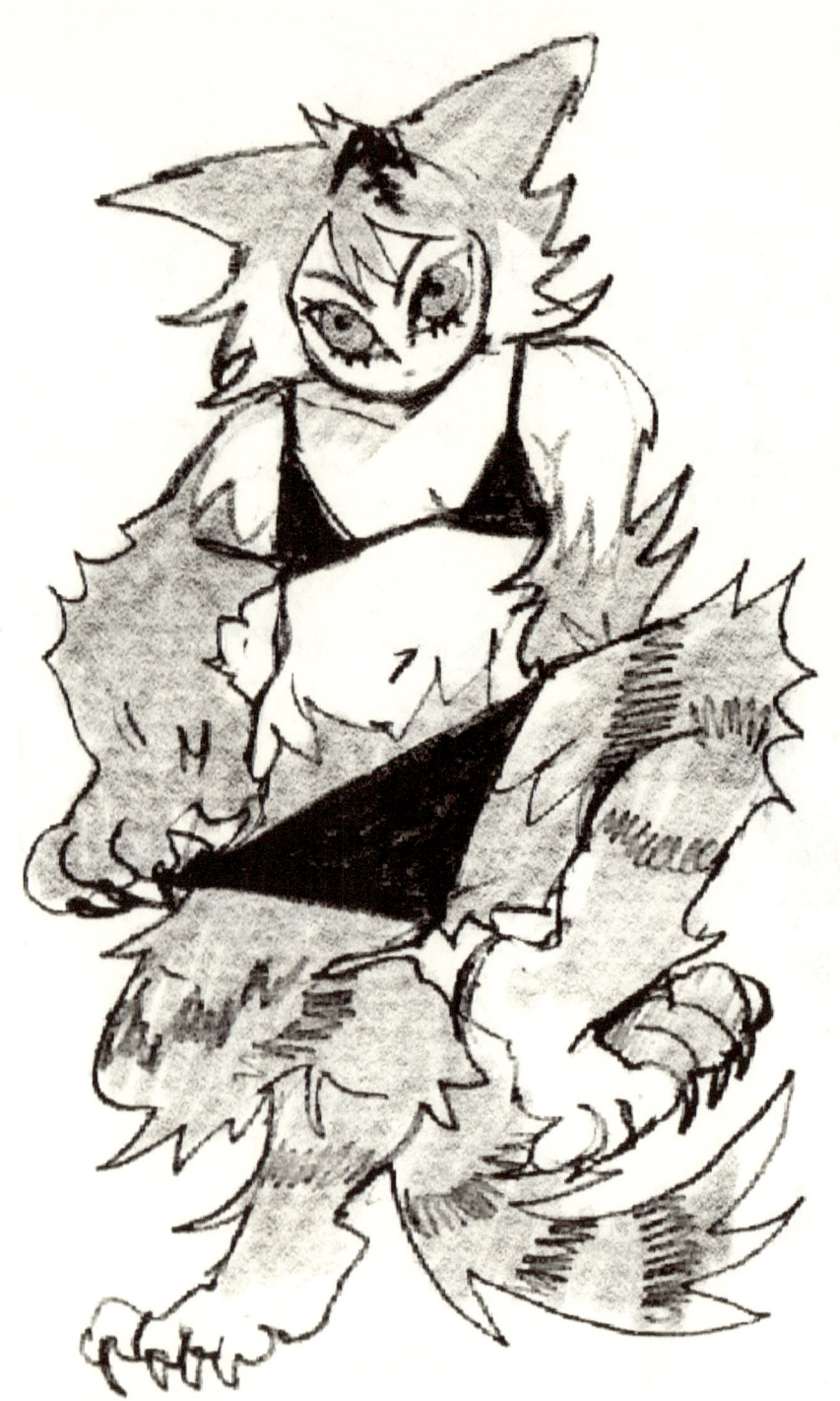

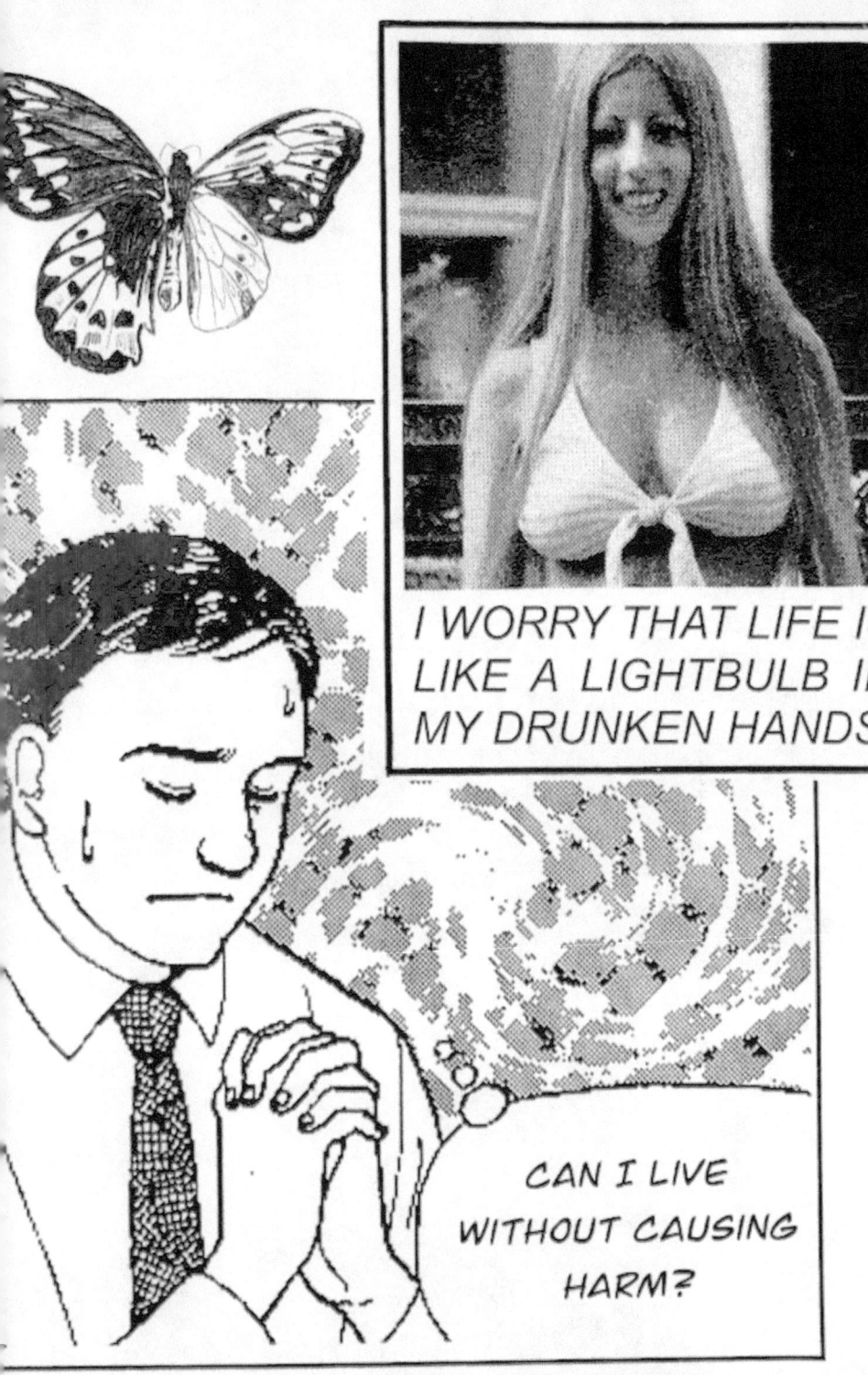

I WORRY THAT LIFE IS LIKE A LIGHTBULB IN MY DRUNKEN HANDS

CAN I LIVE WITHOUT CAUSING HARM?

15

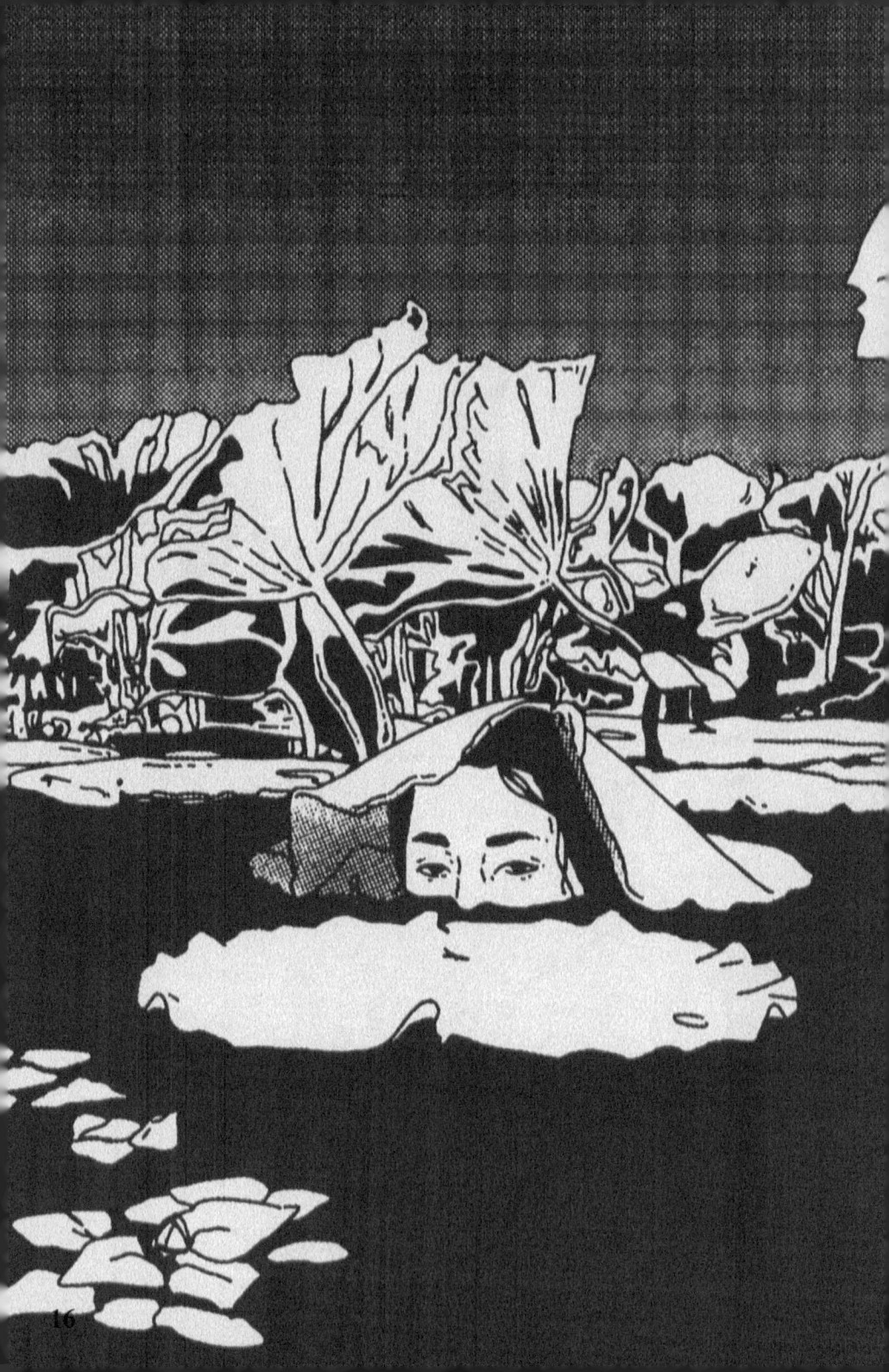

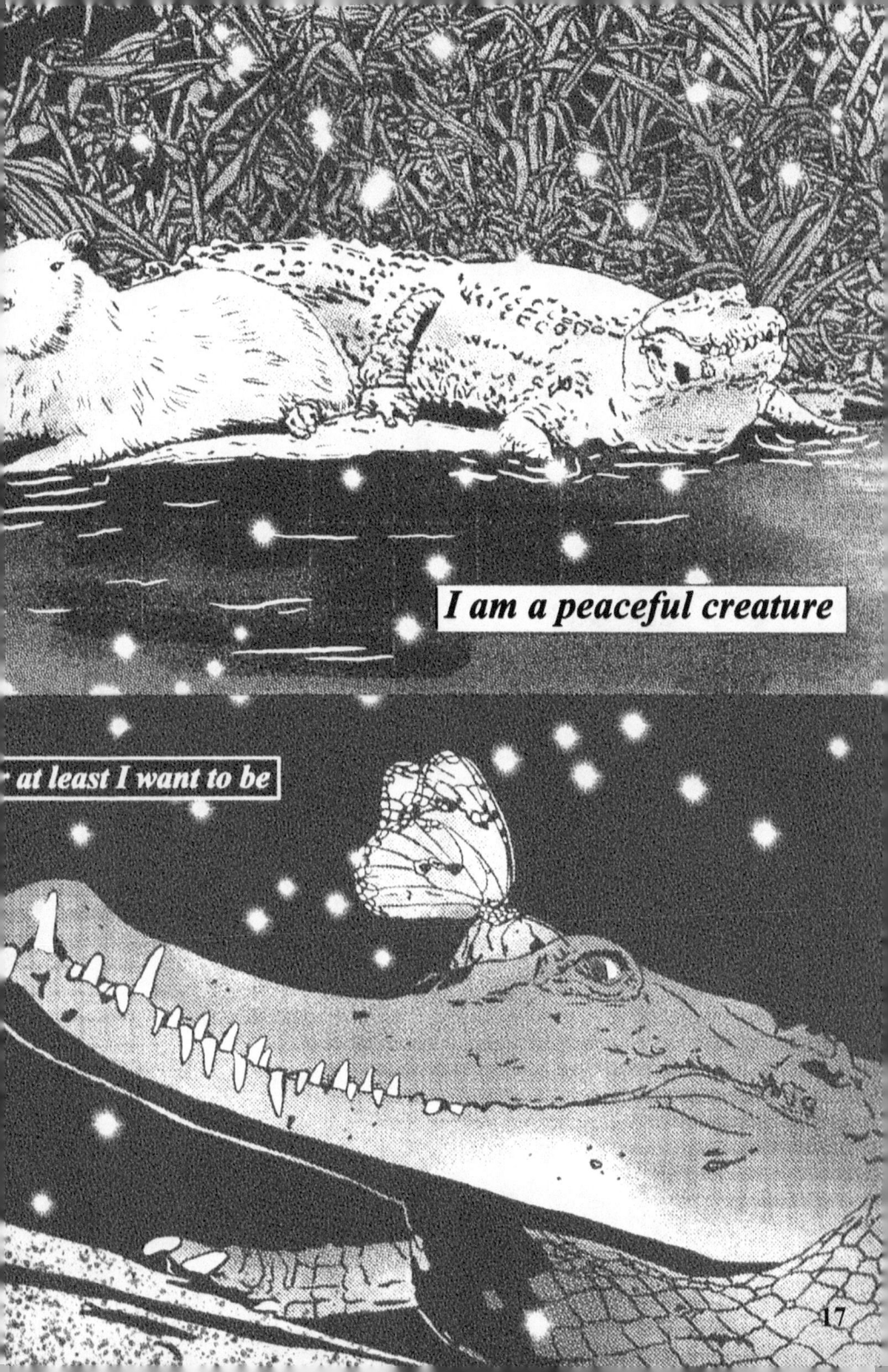

17

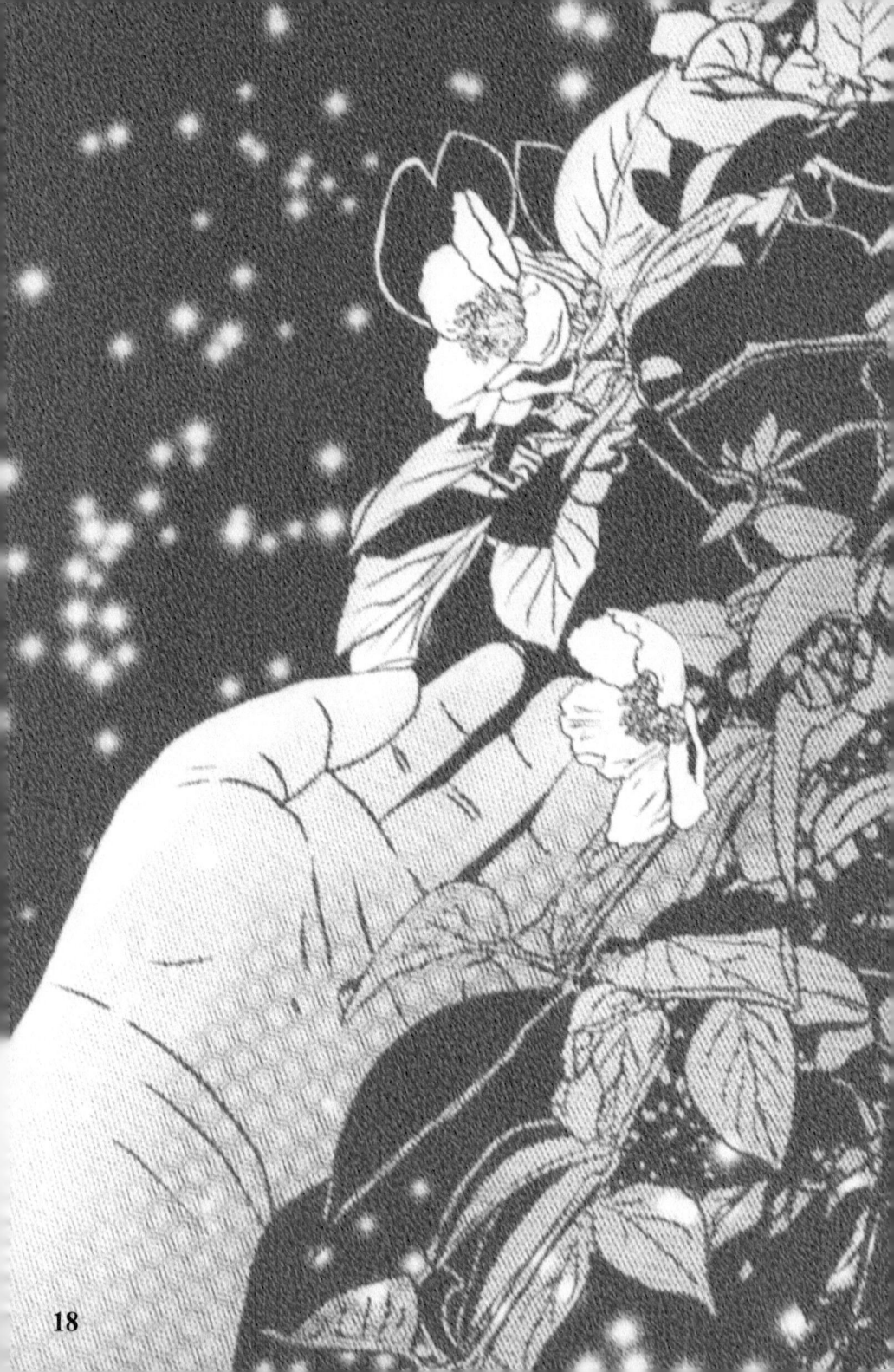

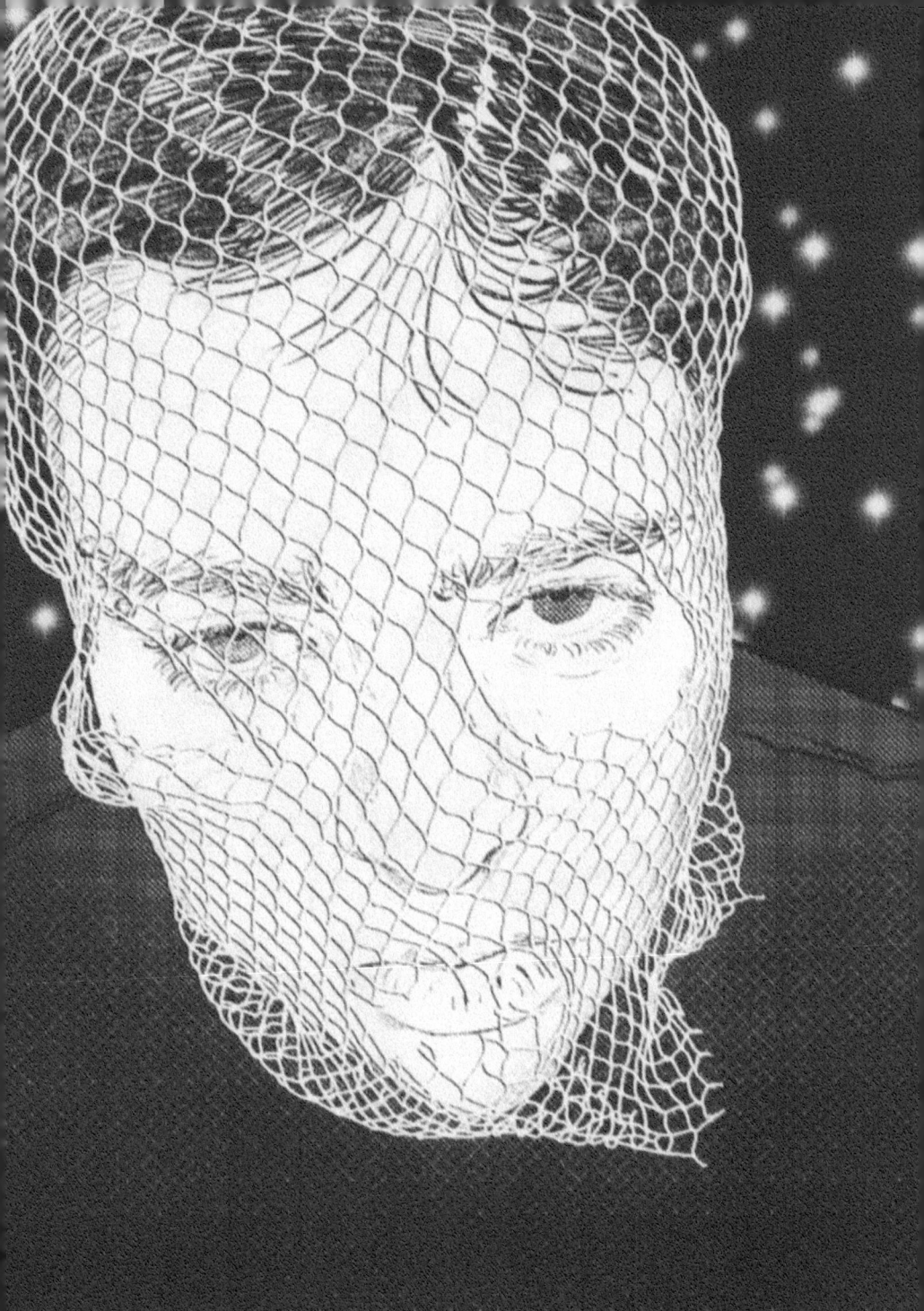

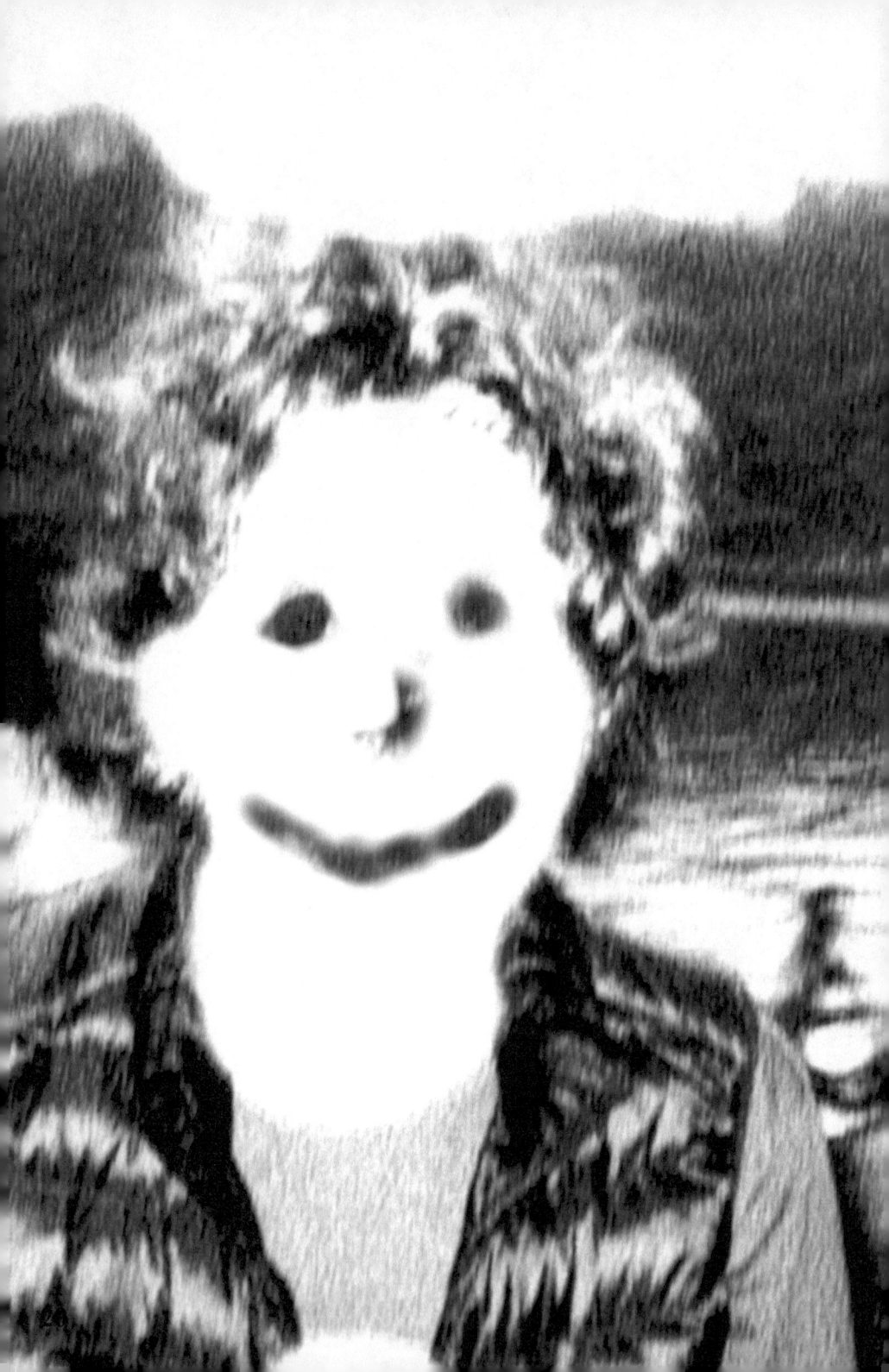

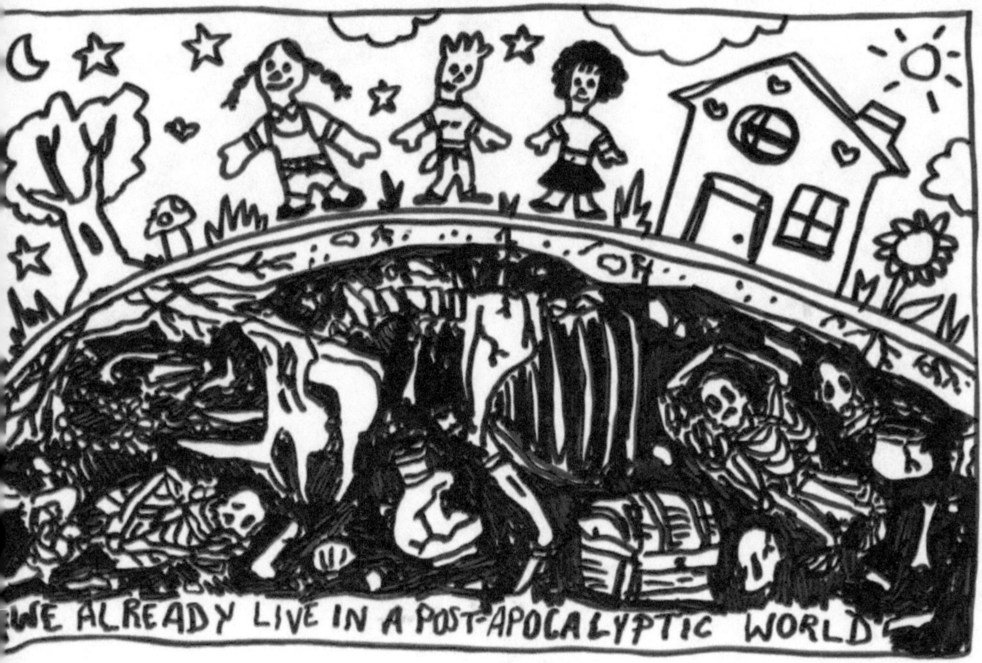

WE ALREADY LIVE IN A POST-APOCALYPTIC WORLD

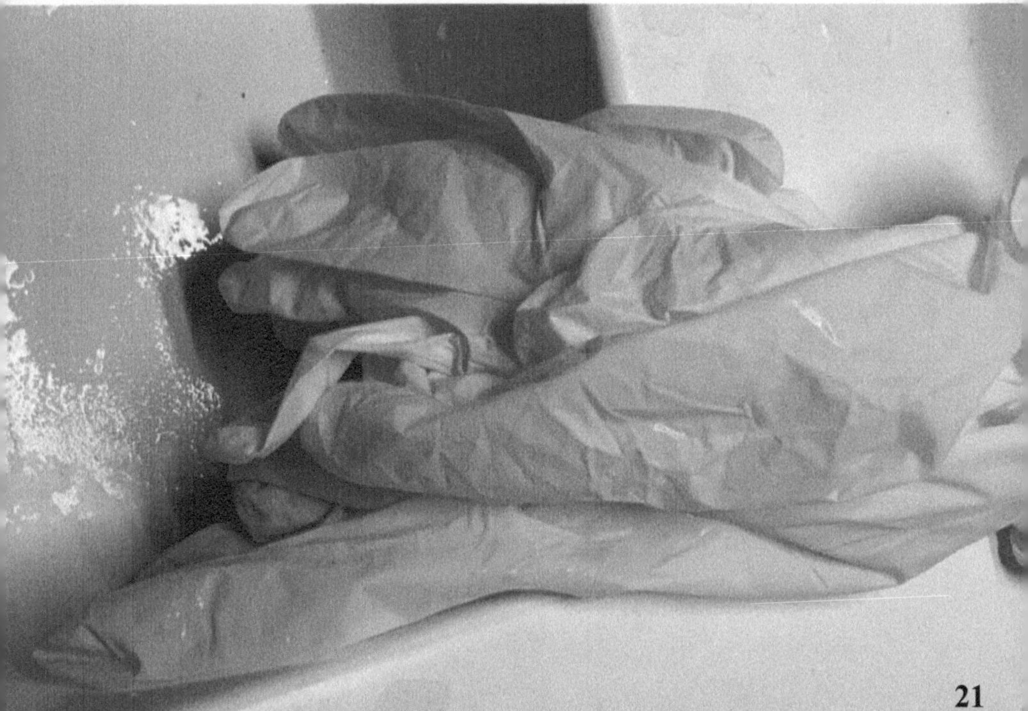

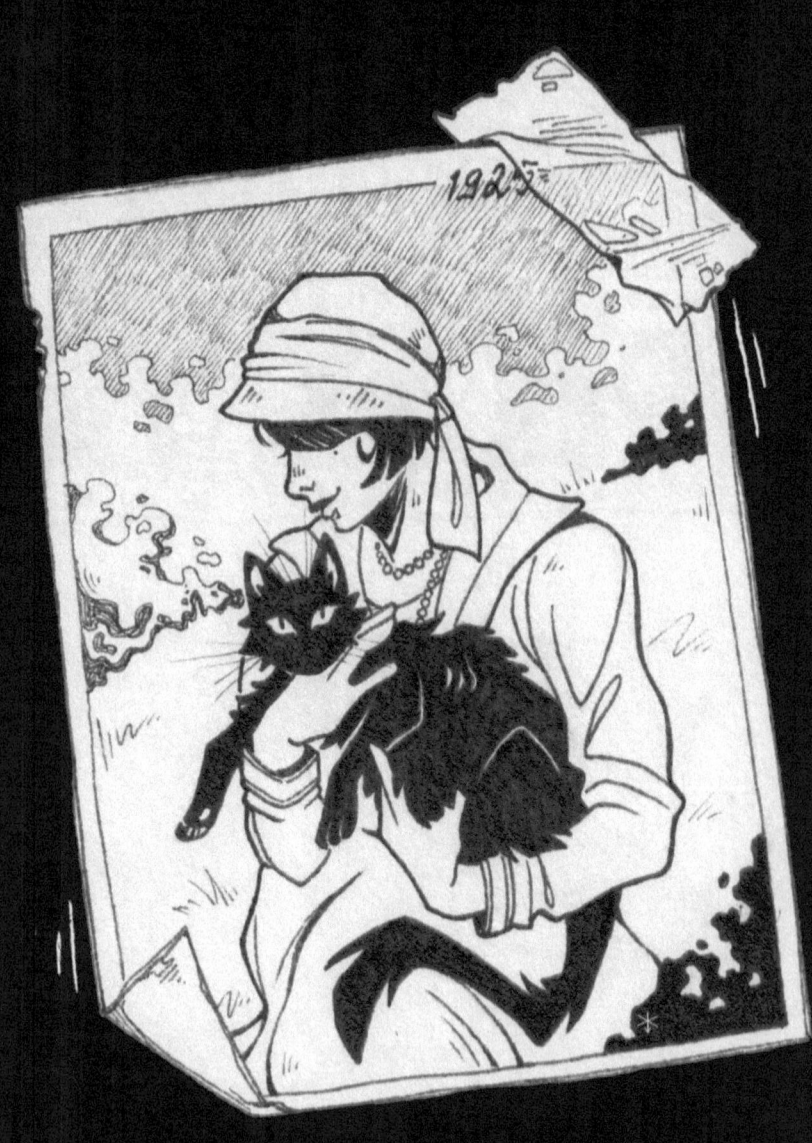

There's a certain
time every year
when
everything that
seemed to be going
easy
begins to feel like
it's falling apart

Beginning of
October–I can't
wear a sweater, not
every day
I'm going to keep
doing whatever it is
that I do
that makes You not
want to go away

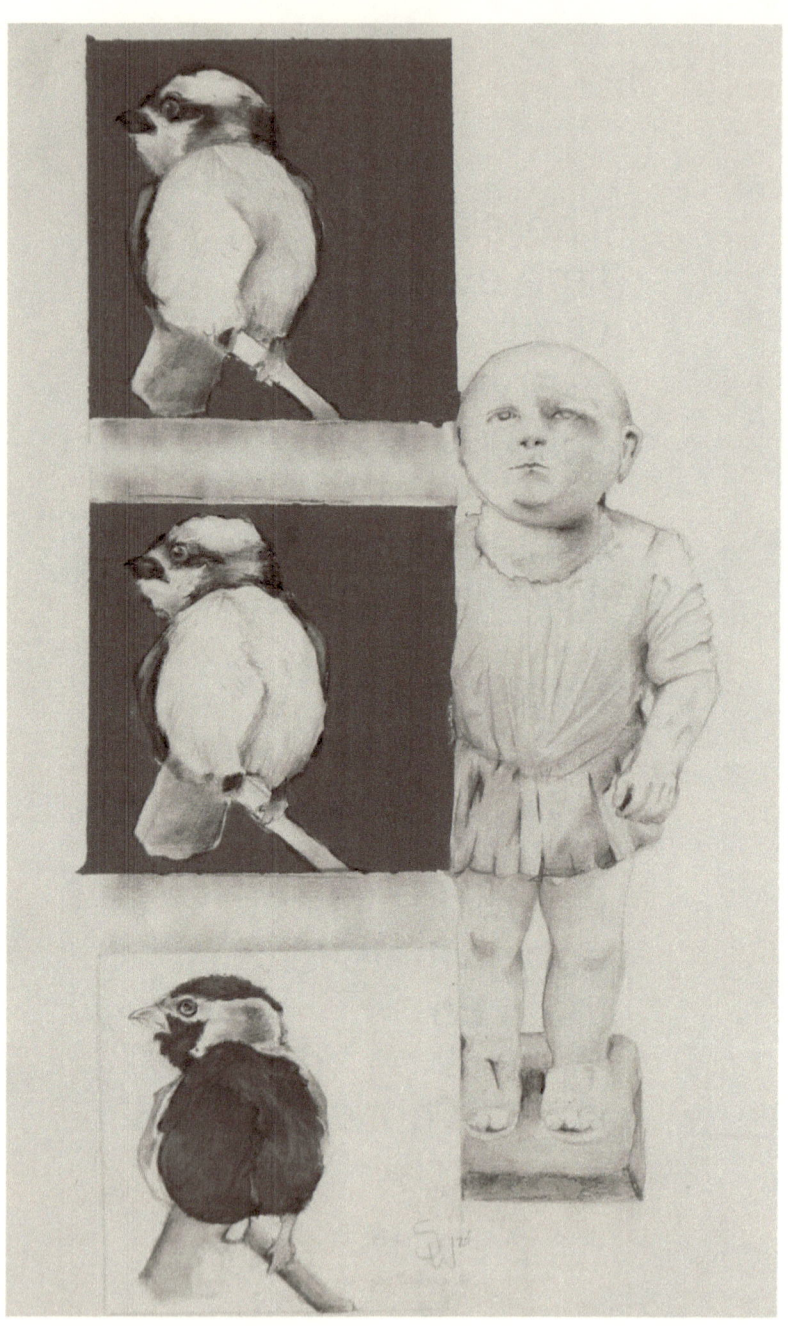

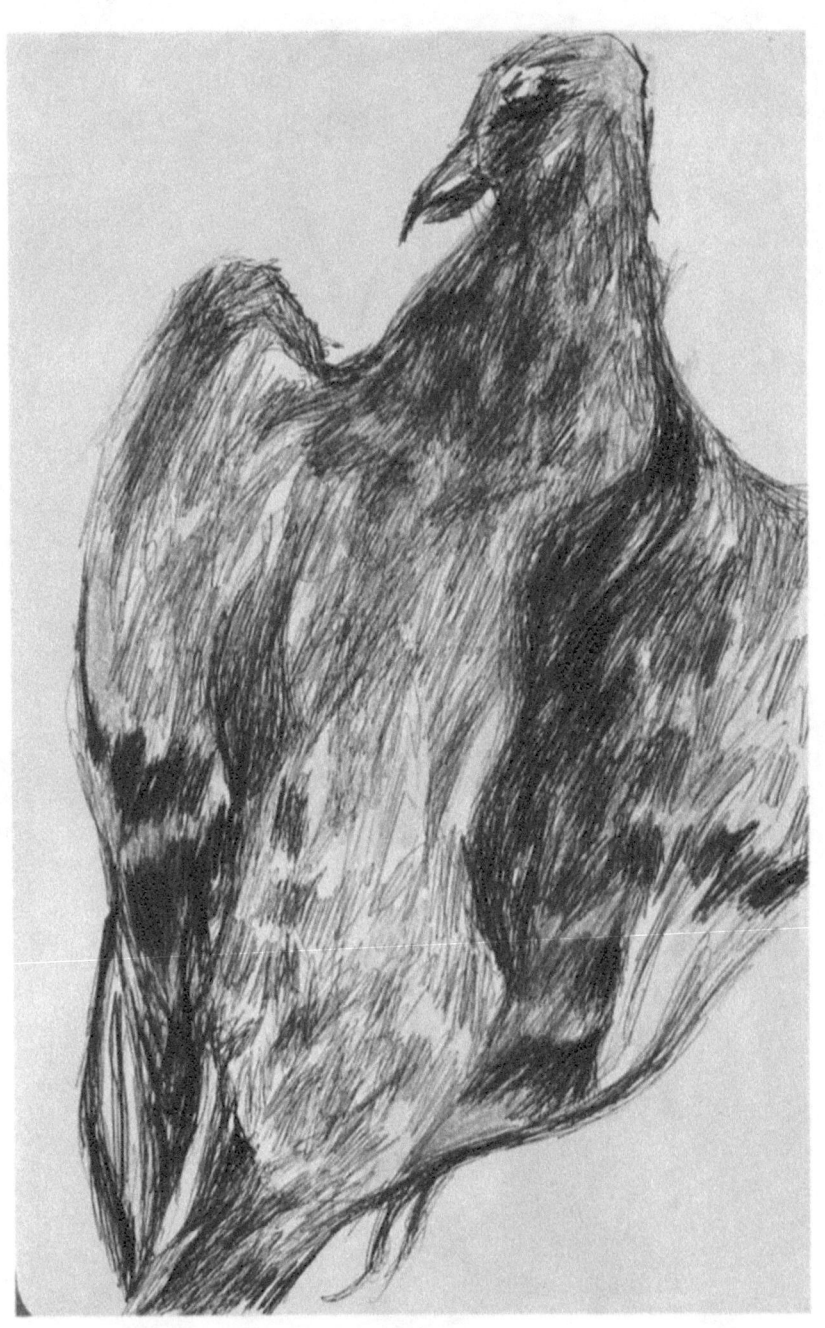

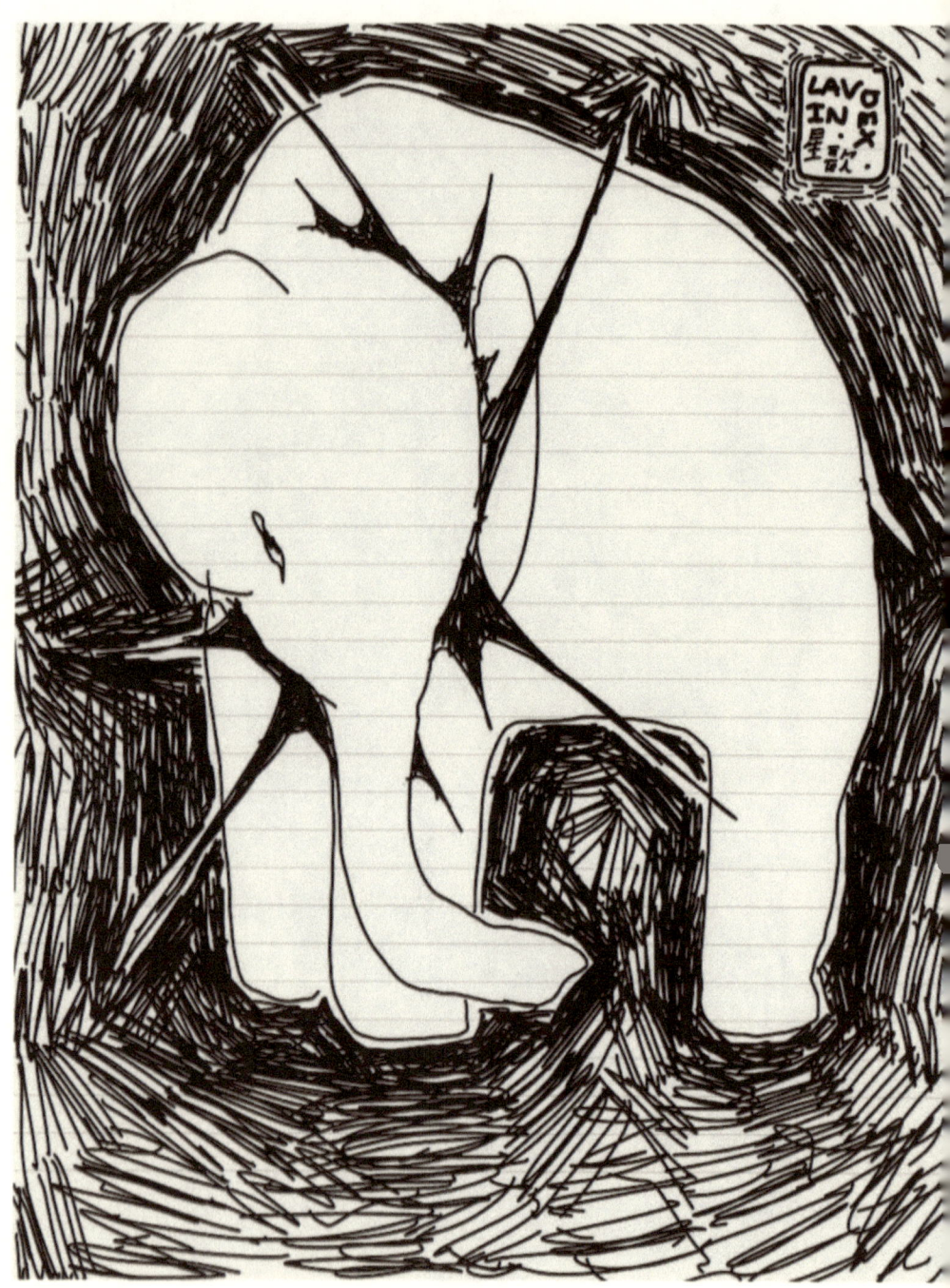

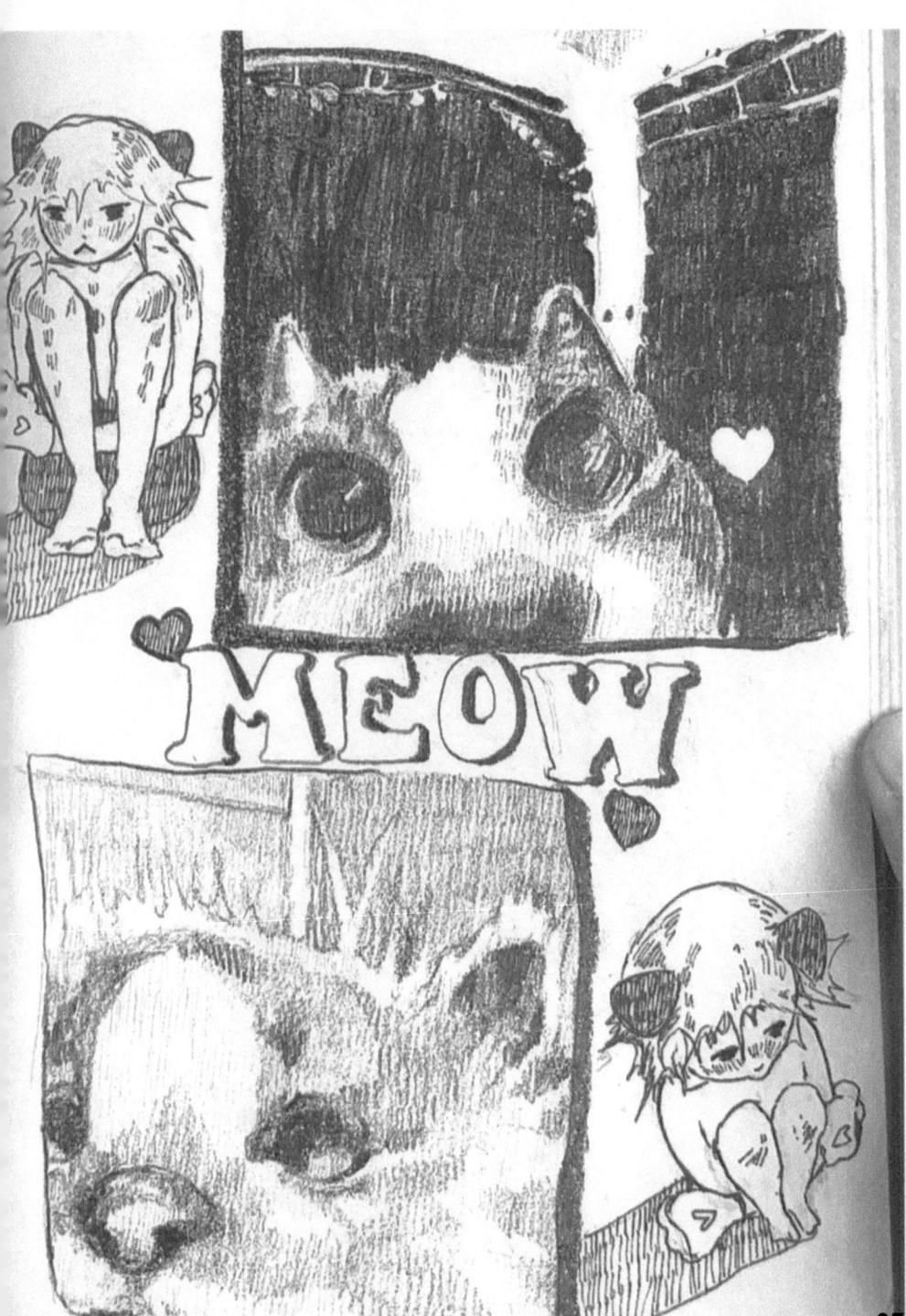

I hold in my hand...

my hand.

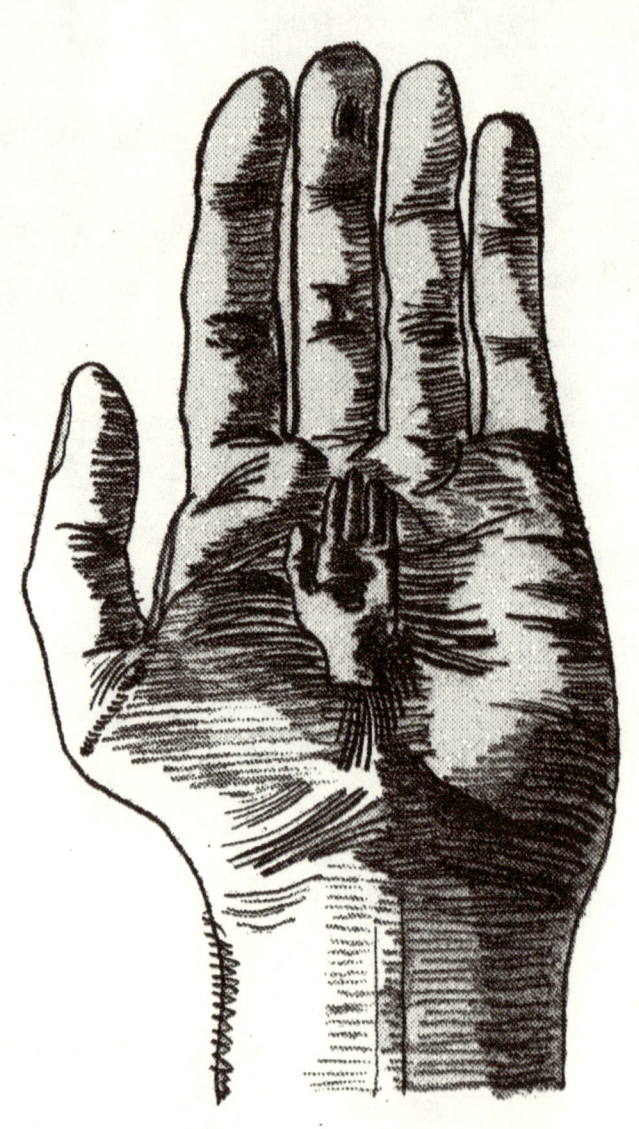

Paraphernalia

jetlagged worm greets me
hair-trigger excerpts
found after crossed out eyes
only my stuff remains
i hope it finds an owner
or a comfy landfill

octopus head abandons me
goodbye little thingy
you will be missed,
but had you stayed
i would mutate into you
and i've grown to dislike
the smell of ink quite a lot
makes me icky and begrimed

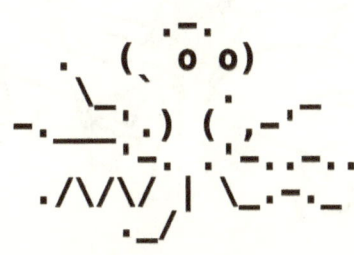

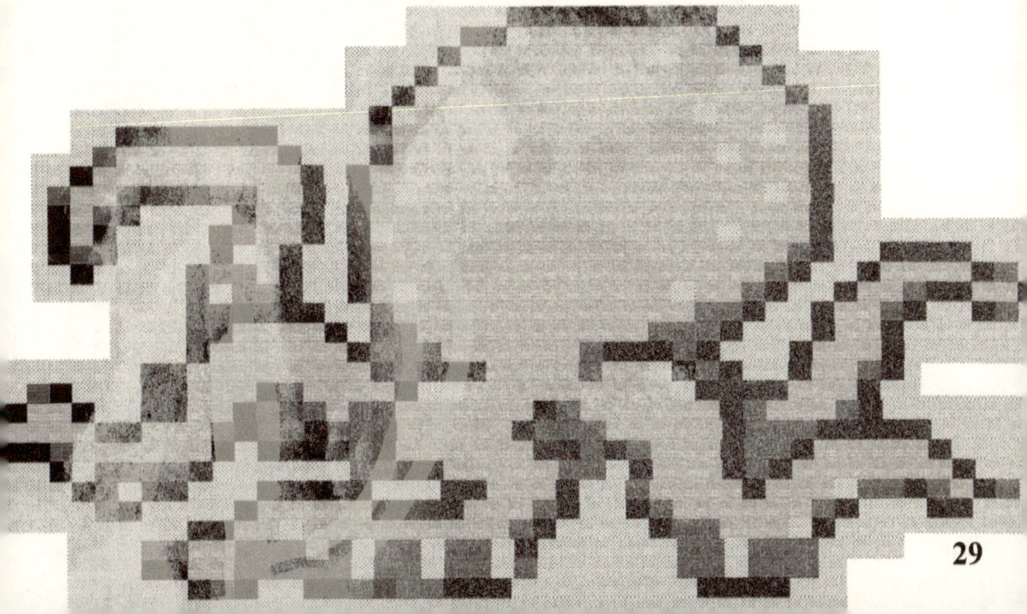

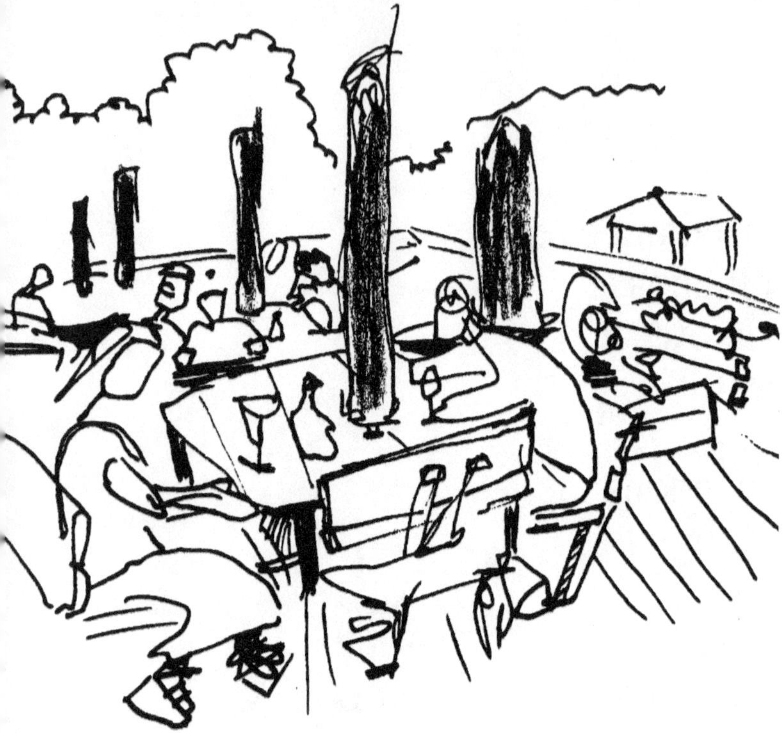

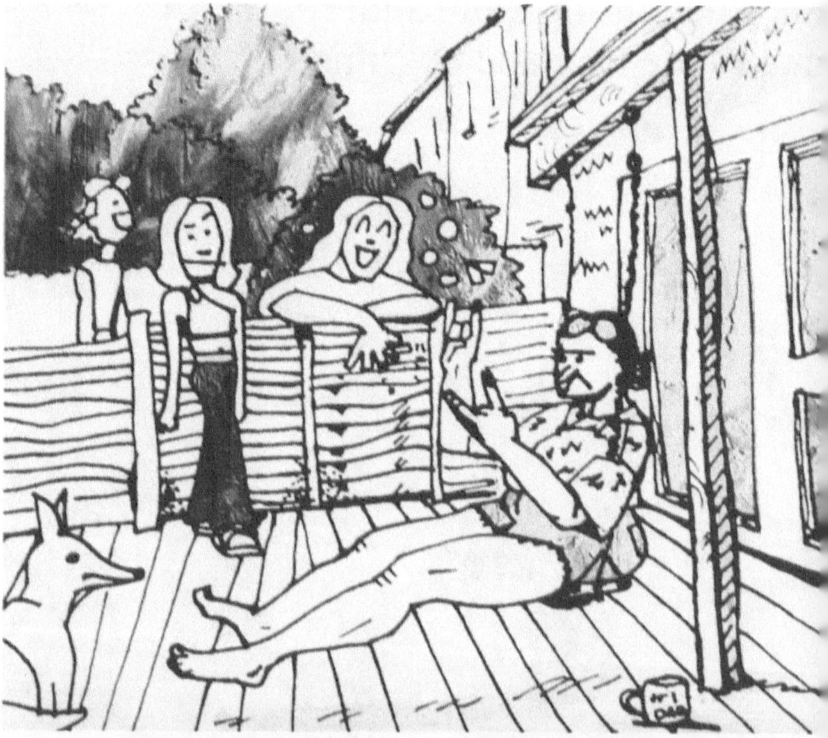

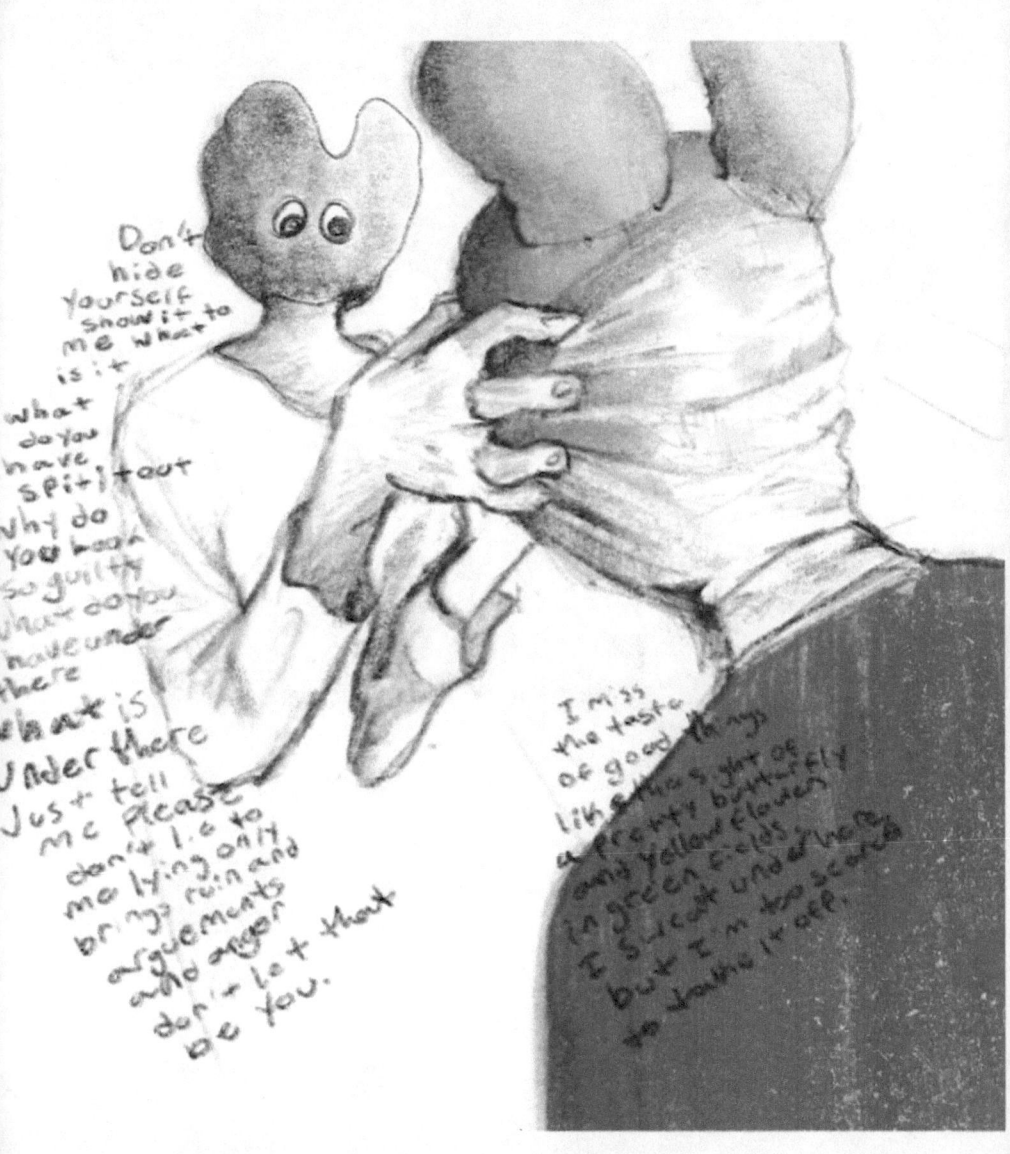

Don't hide yourself show it to me what to is it

what do you have spit it out

why do you look so guilty what do you have under there

what is under there

Just tell me please don't lie to me lying only brings ruin and arguements and anger don't let that be you.

I miss the taste of good things like the sight of a pretty butterfly and yellow flowers in green fields, I see it under here but I'm too scared to take it off.

SIX DEGREES

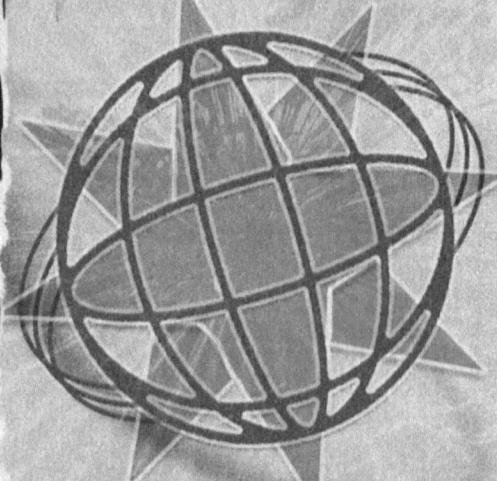

EVEN THOUGH THE WORLD BARELY RECOGNIZES

SINGULAR EXISTENCE

HUMANS ARE SO SELF ABSORBED.

OF SEPARATION

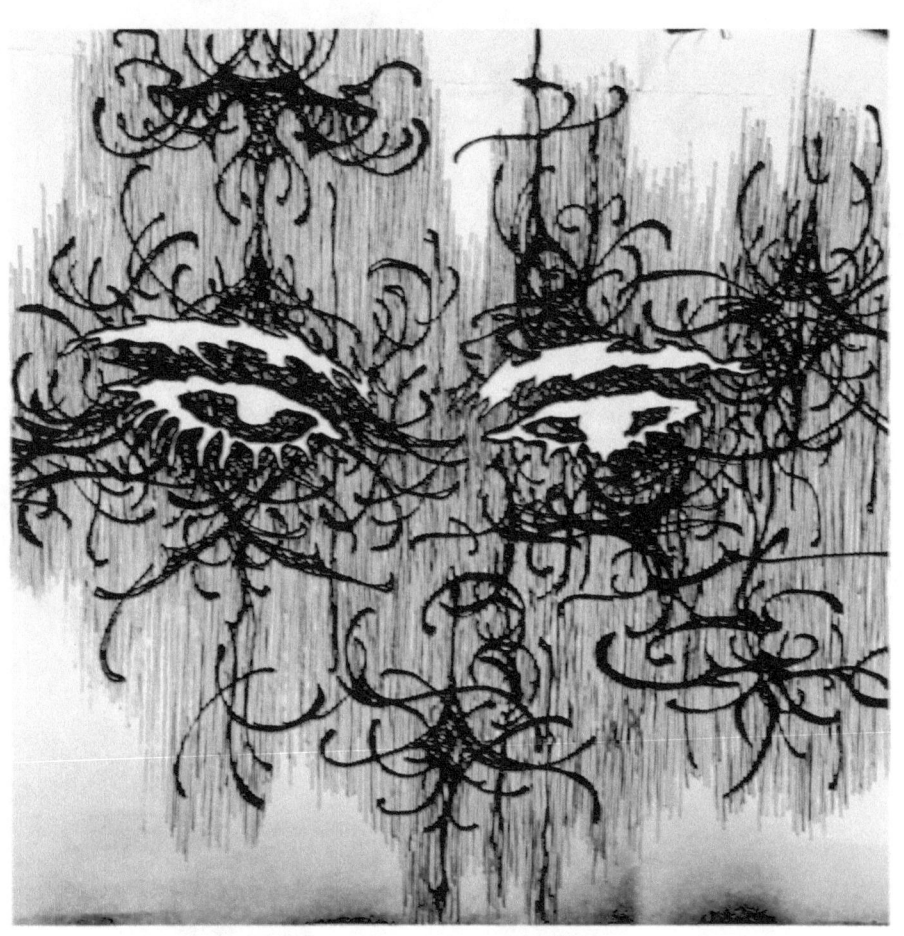

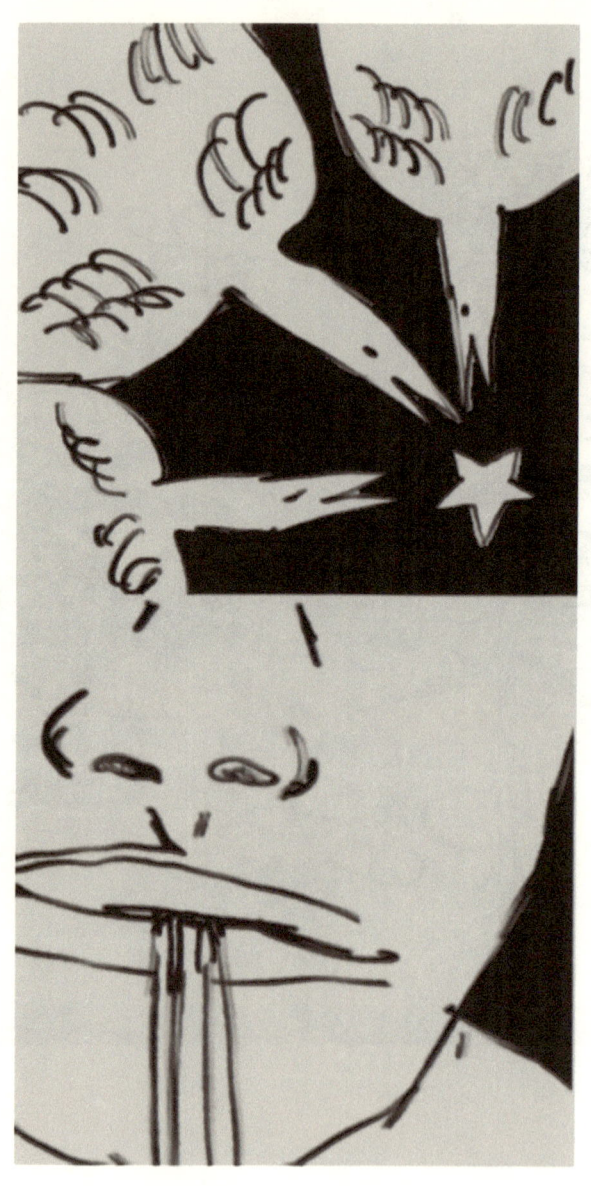

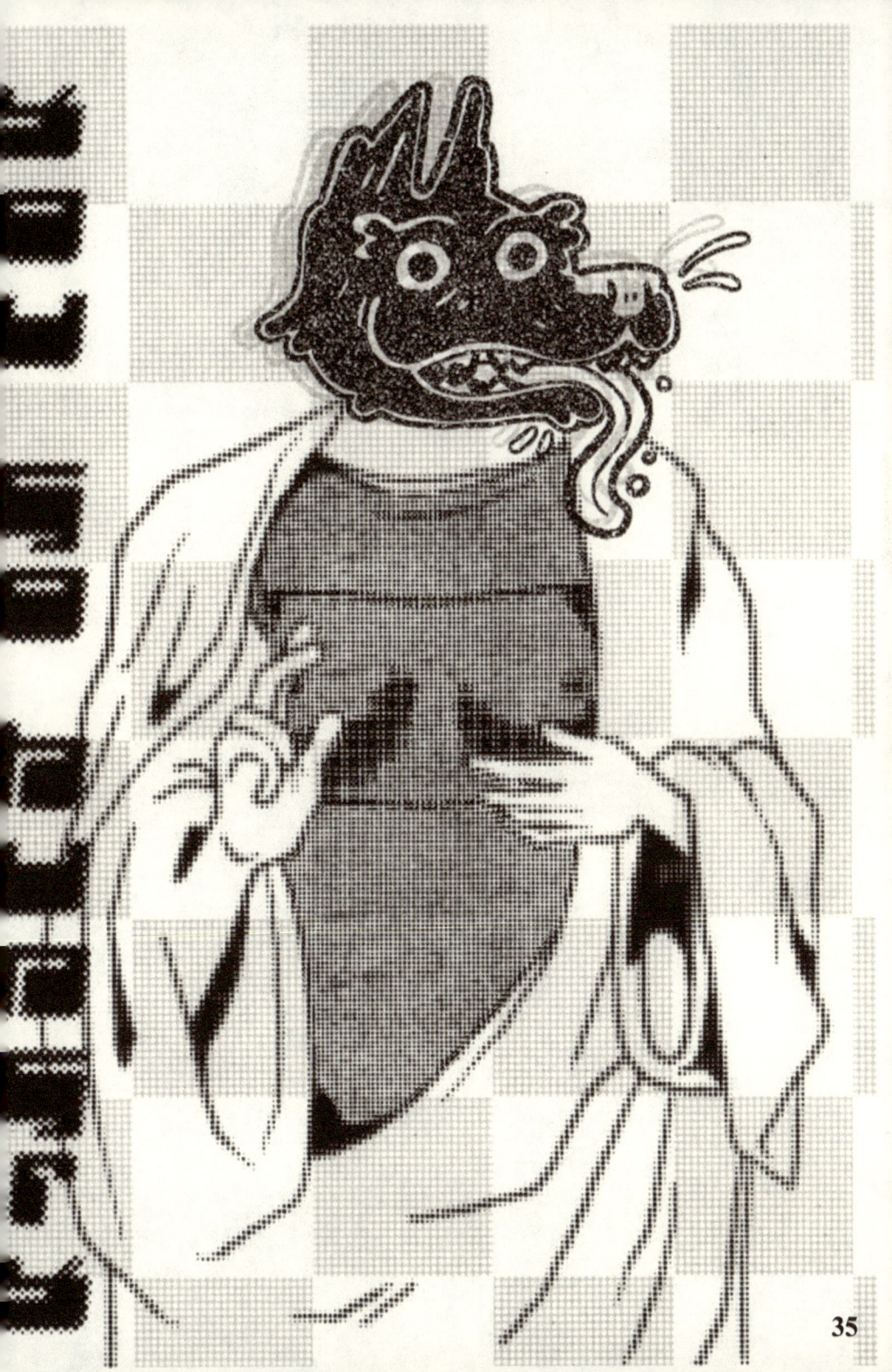

35

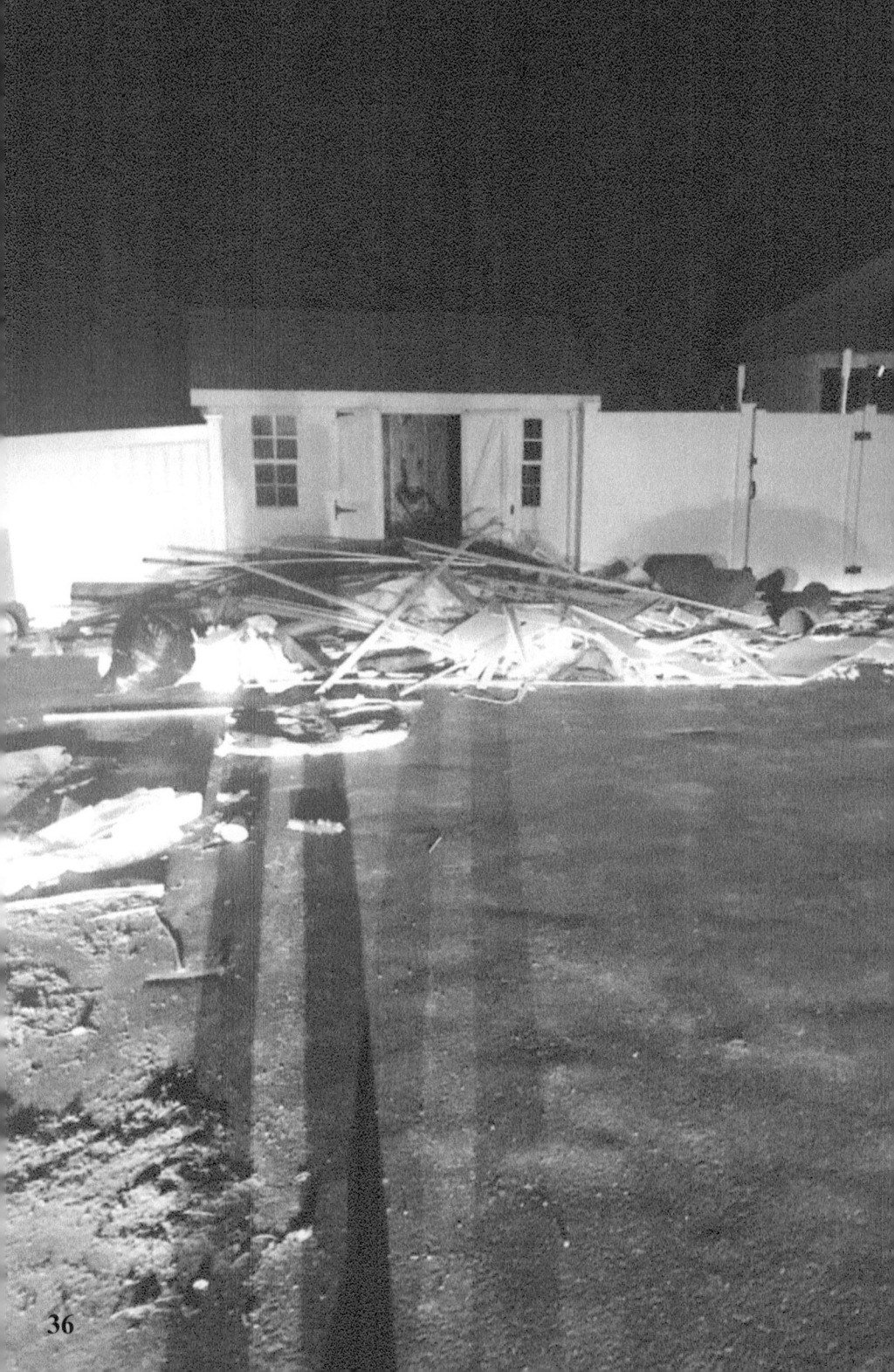

2:25 AM

A cold Christmas eve at 11:59 PM
I am sitting at my desk doing homework
When a minute later "tick tock"
The clock chimes midnight
I retreat upstairs
Unknowingly walking past the firelight that
set my house alight at 2:25 AM
It only took a spark in which a dark house
became a candle for the whole block to see
But I didn't see the spark
I didn't see my house burn alive in the dark
I didn't hear the panic in my family's voices
as they ran out and apart
From the house set aflame at 2:25 AM
I laid there in the darkness of my sheets
I stayed in the burning house
asleep, at peace, dormant
Until it was over.

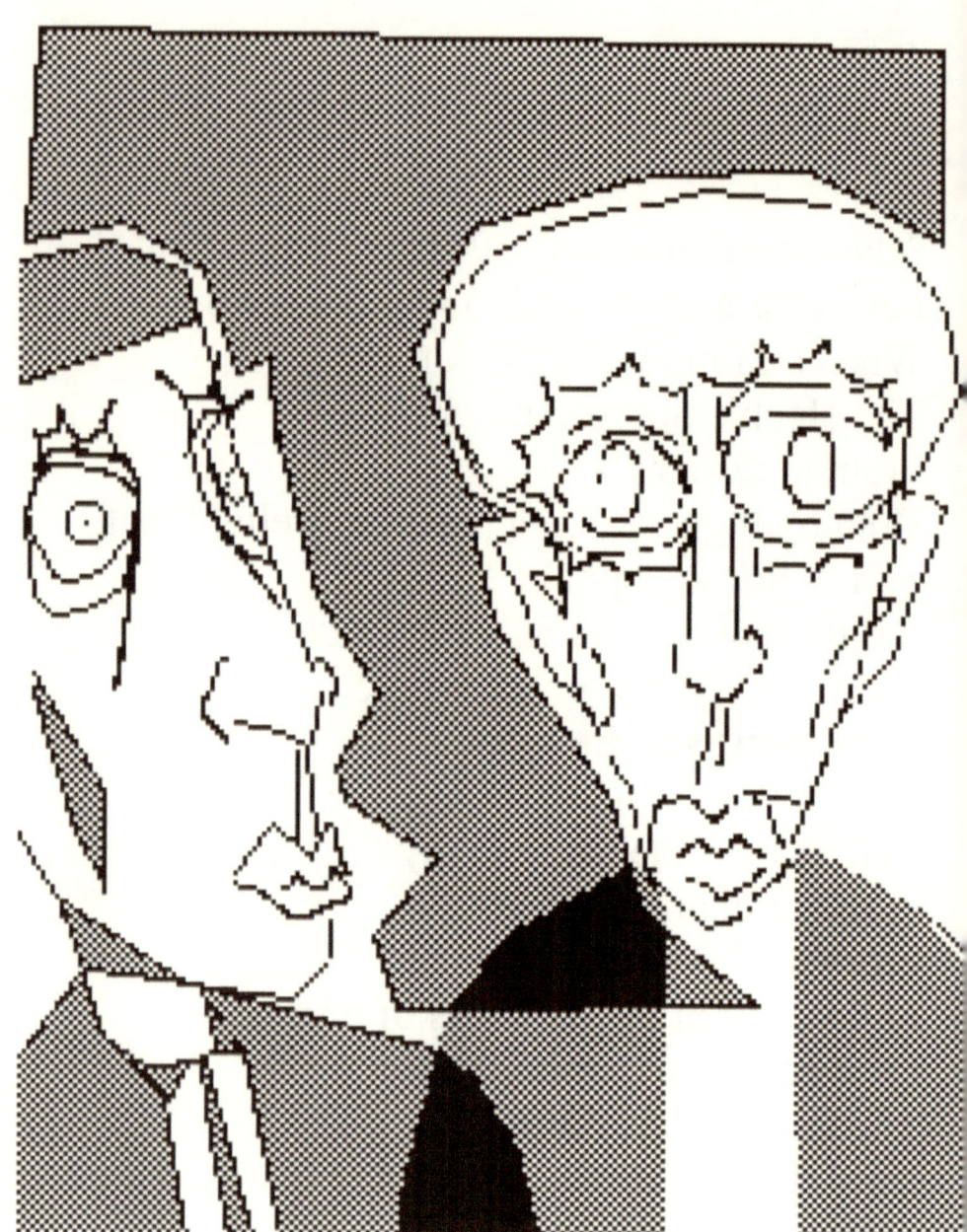

The Aftermath of 2:25 AM

I awake not of my own accord
But from the brightness of a flashlight
The harsh light shot into my eyes
It woke me from my slumber in the flames
I walk outside the consumed house at 2:53
AM
I witness the multiple firetrucks and curious
neighbors overlooking our house
I witnessed so much of the insurance
battles, the rumors, the facebook posts,
And the burnt remains of 2:25 AM

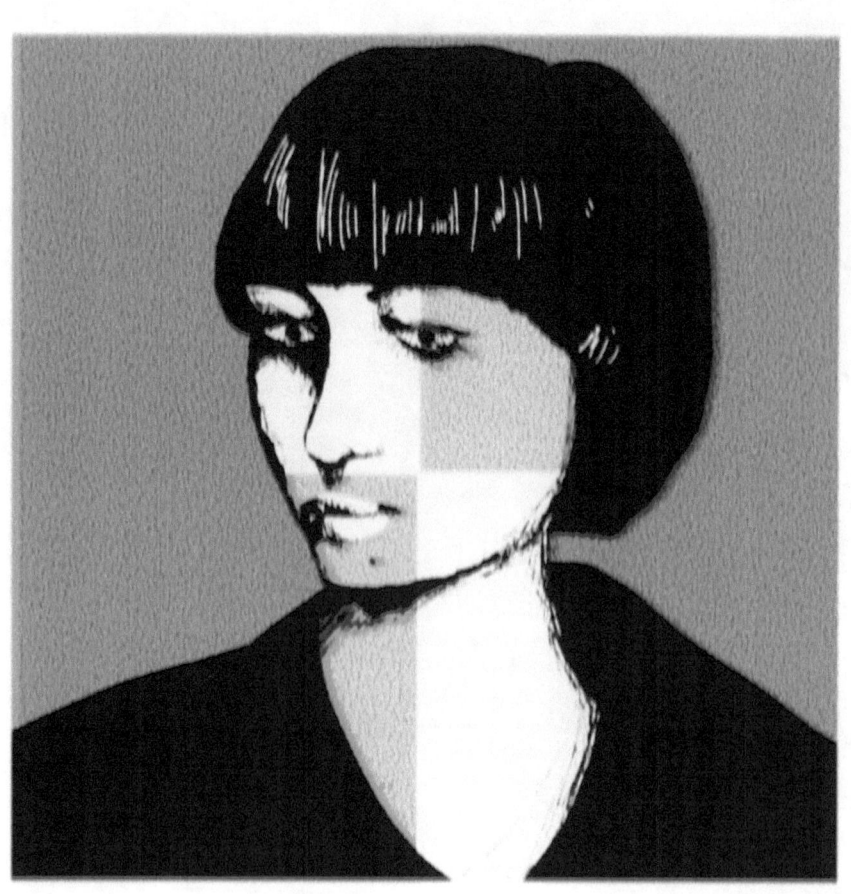

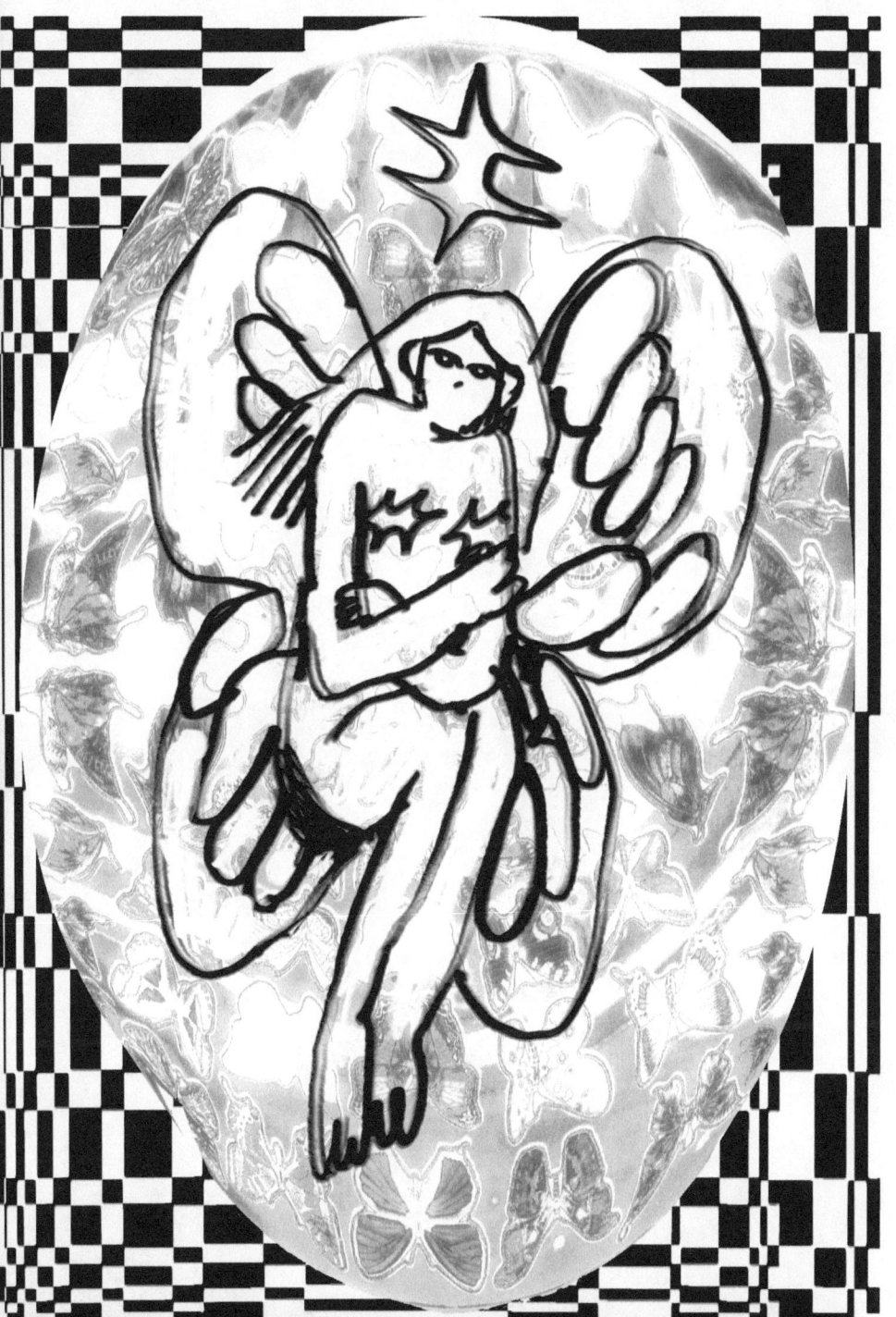

43

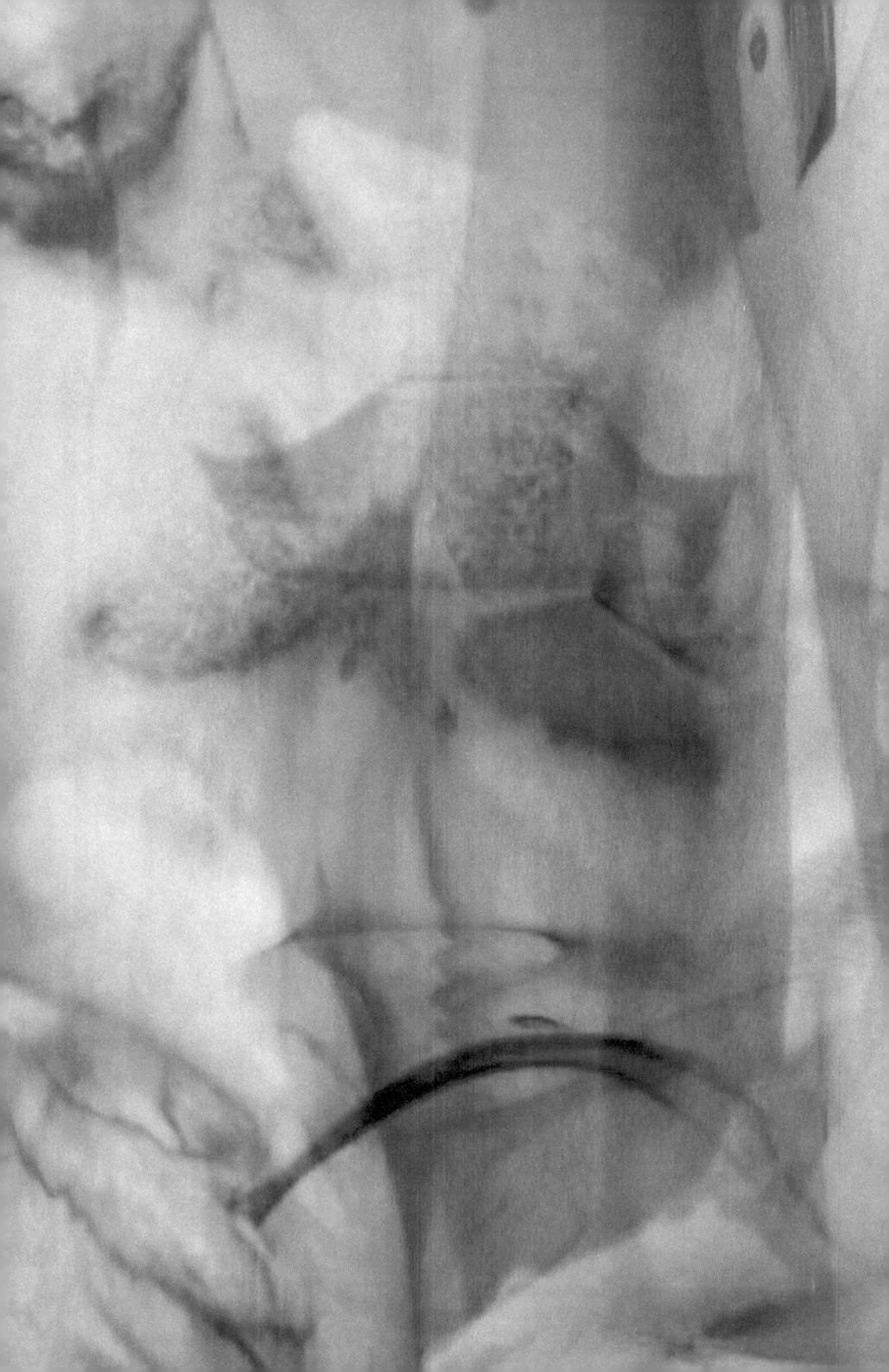

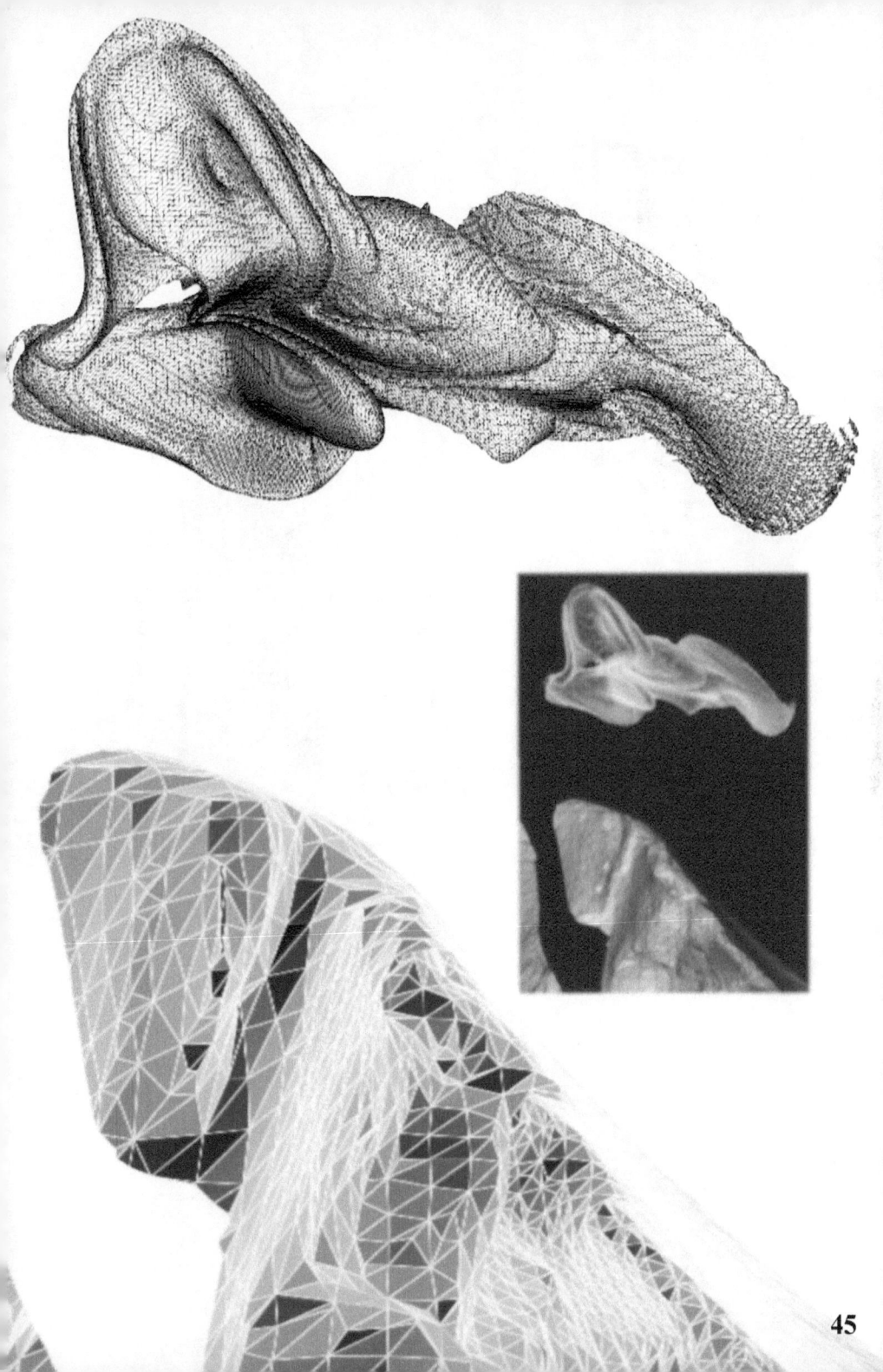

45

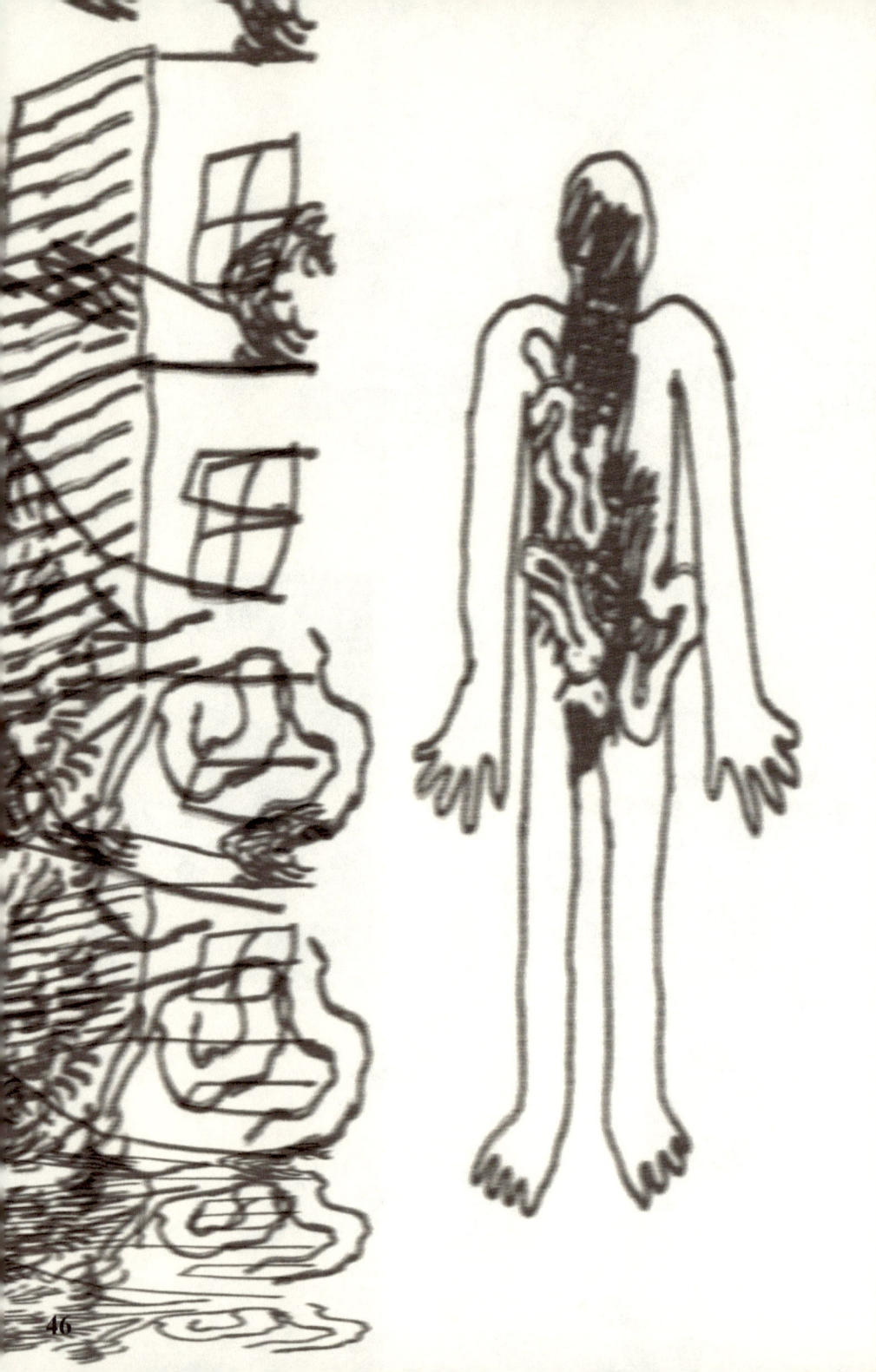

46

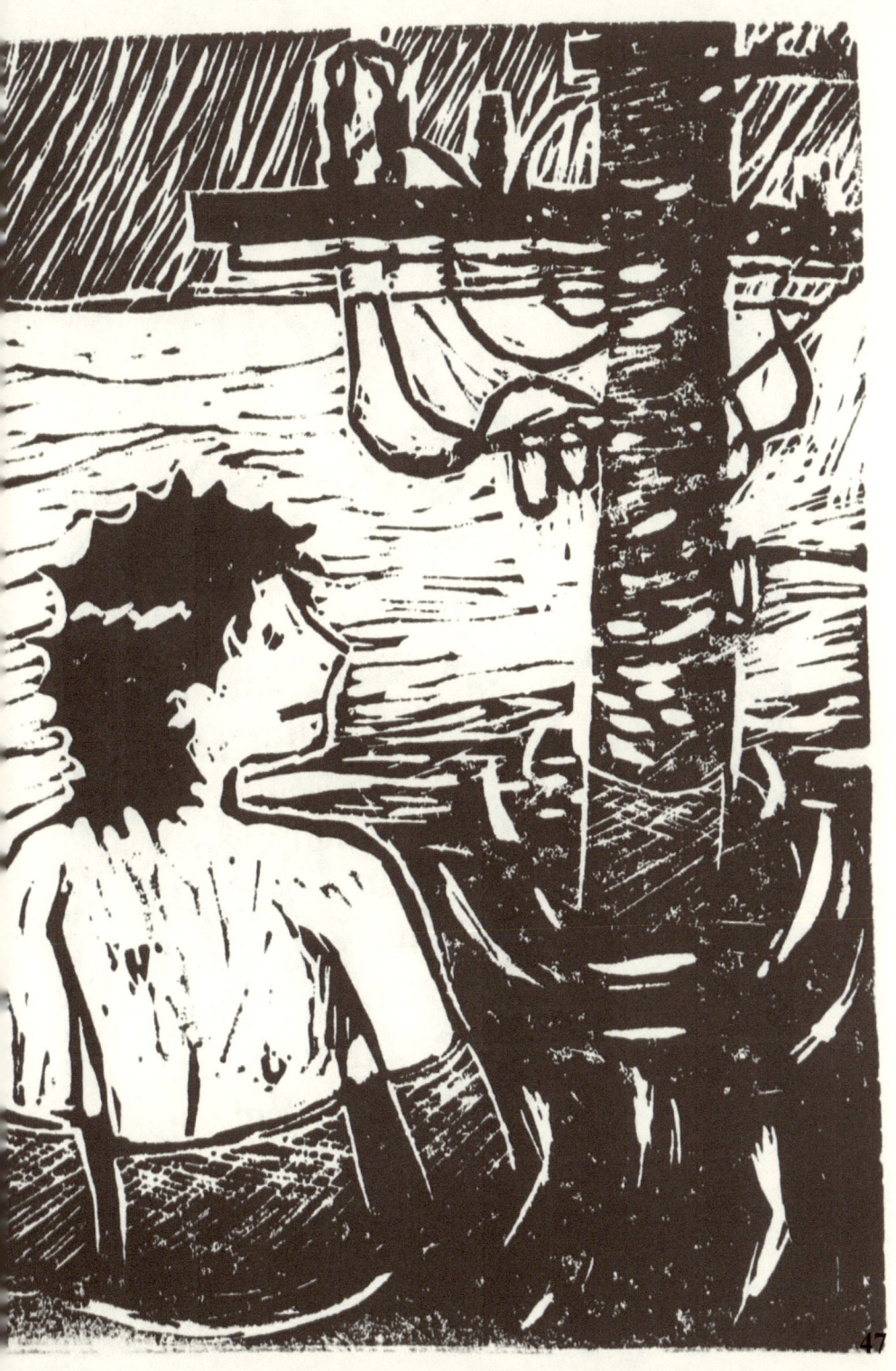

47

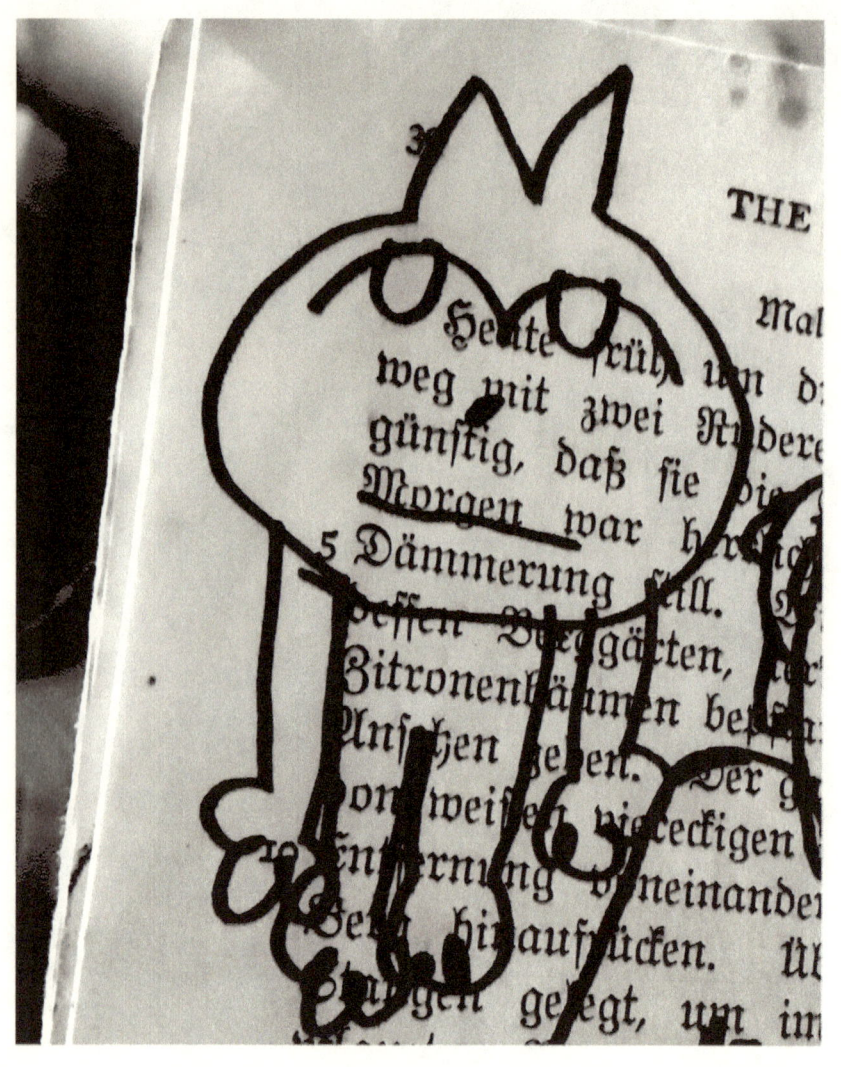

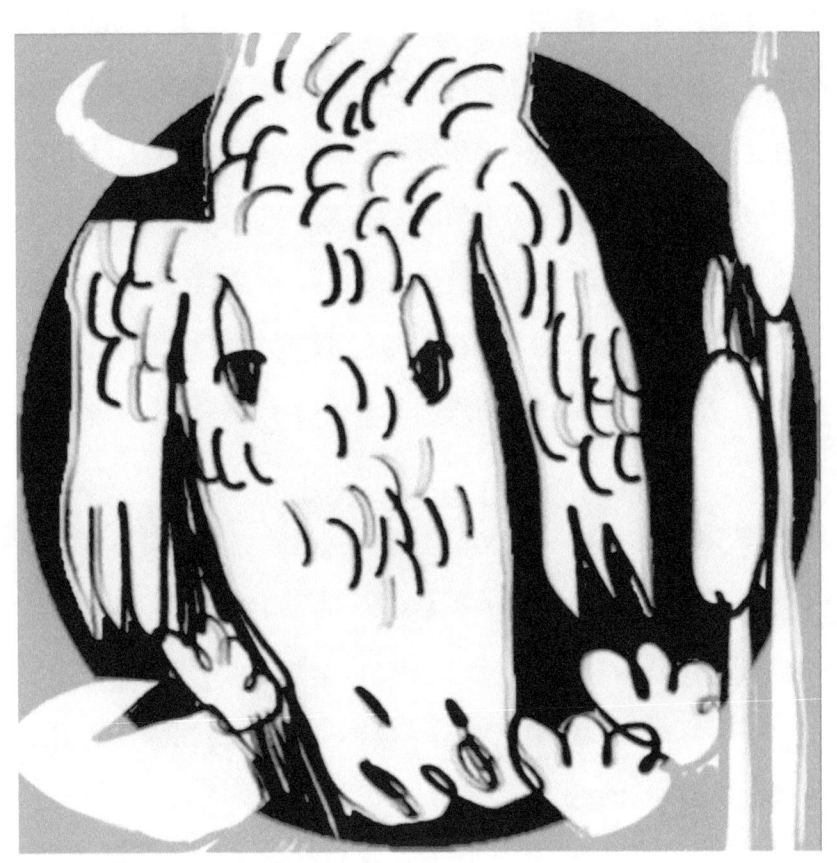

You are an agent of the apocalypse
You are an agent of the apocalypse
You are an agent of the apocalypse
You are an agent of the apocalypse
You are an agent of the apocalypse
You are an agent of the apocalypse
You are an agent of the apocalypse
You are an agent of the apocalypse
You are an agent of the apocalypse
You are an agent of the apocalypse
You are an agent of the apocalypse
You are an agent of the apocalypse

You are an agent of the apocalypse
You are an agent of the apocalypse
You are an agent of the apocalypse
You are an agent of the apocalypse
You are an agent of the apocalypse
You are an agent of the apocalypse
You are an agent of the apocalypse
You are an agent of the apocalypse
You are an agent of the apocalypse
You are an agent of the apocalypse
You are an agent of the apocalypse

You are an agent of the apocalypse

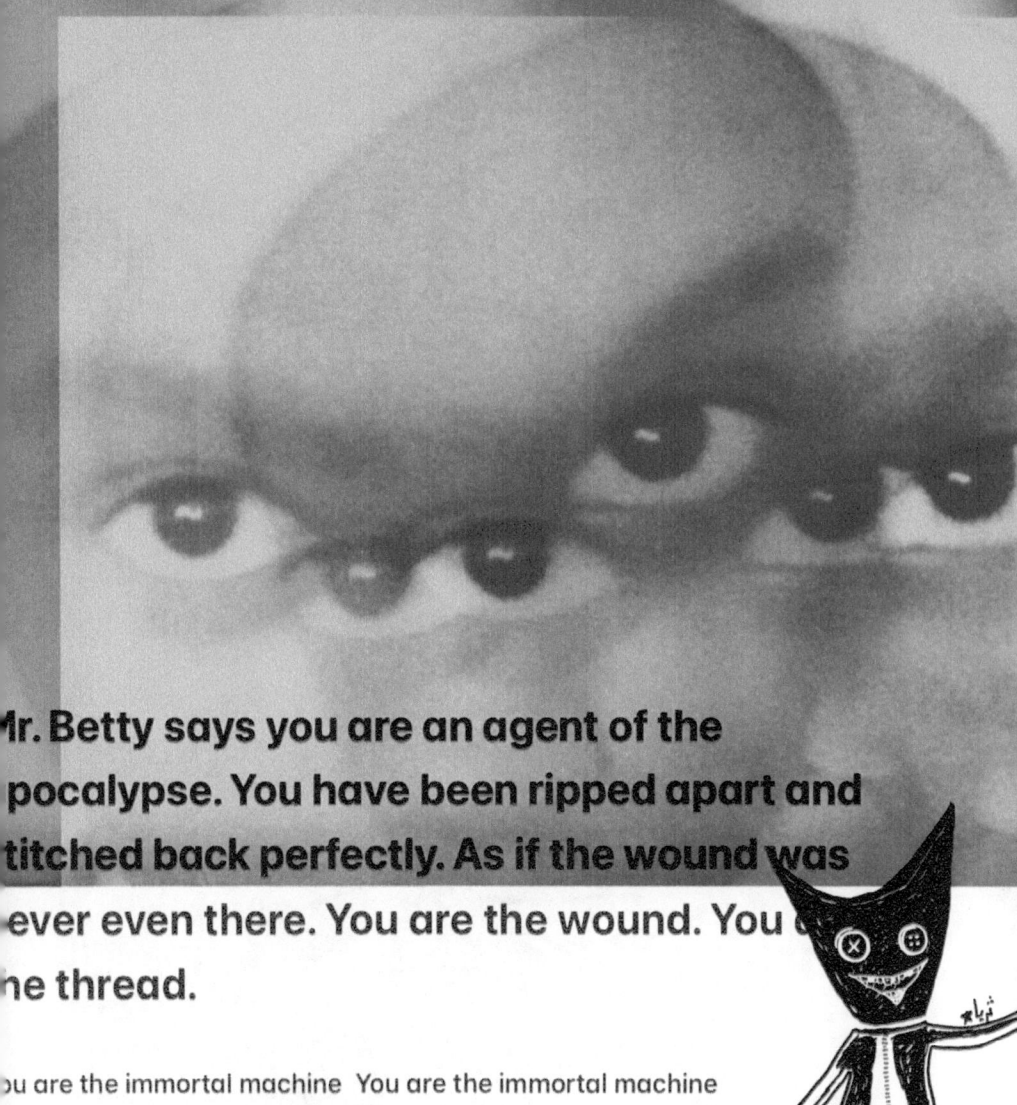

Mr. Betty says you are an agent of the
pocalypse. You have been ripped apart and
titched back perfectly. As if the wound was
ever even there. You are the wound. You
he thread.

ou are the immortal machine   You are the immortal machine
ou are the immortal machine   You are the immortal machine
ou are the immortal machine   You are the immortal machine
ou are the immortal machine   You are the immortal machine
ou are the immortal machine   You are the immortal machine
ou are the immortal machine   You are the immortal machine
ou are the immortal machine   You are the immortal machine
ou are the immortal machine   You are the immortal machine
ou are the immortal machine   You are the immortal machine
ou are the immortal machine   You are the immortal machine
ou are the immortal machine   You are the immortal machine
ou are the immortal machine   You are the immortal machine

51

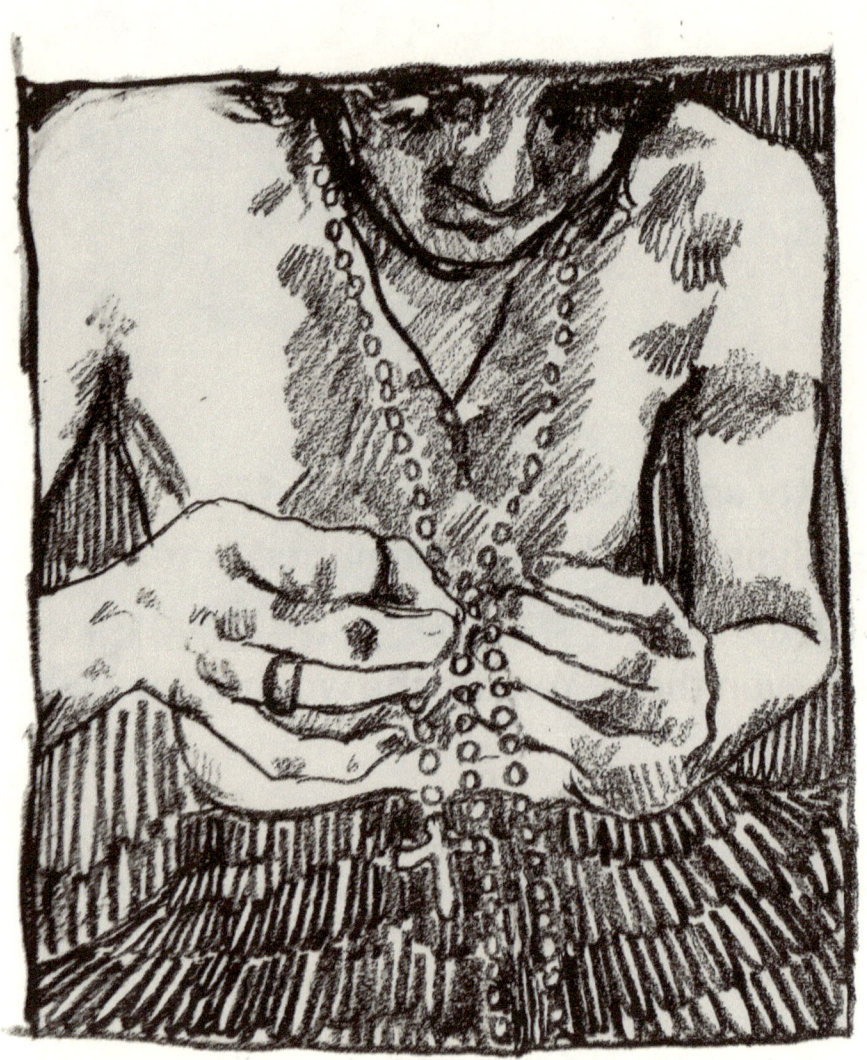

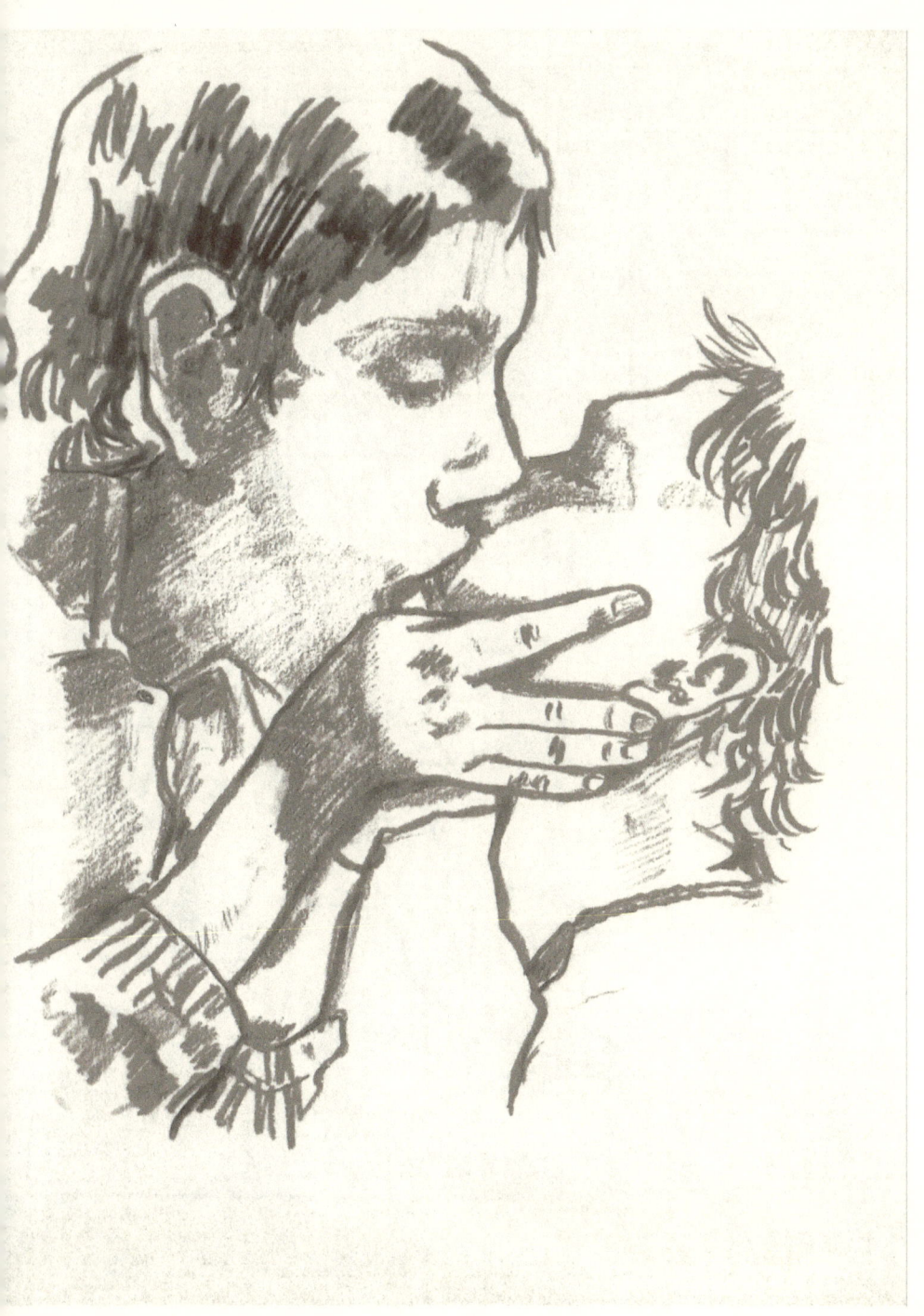

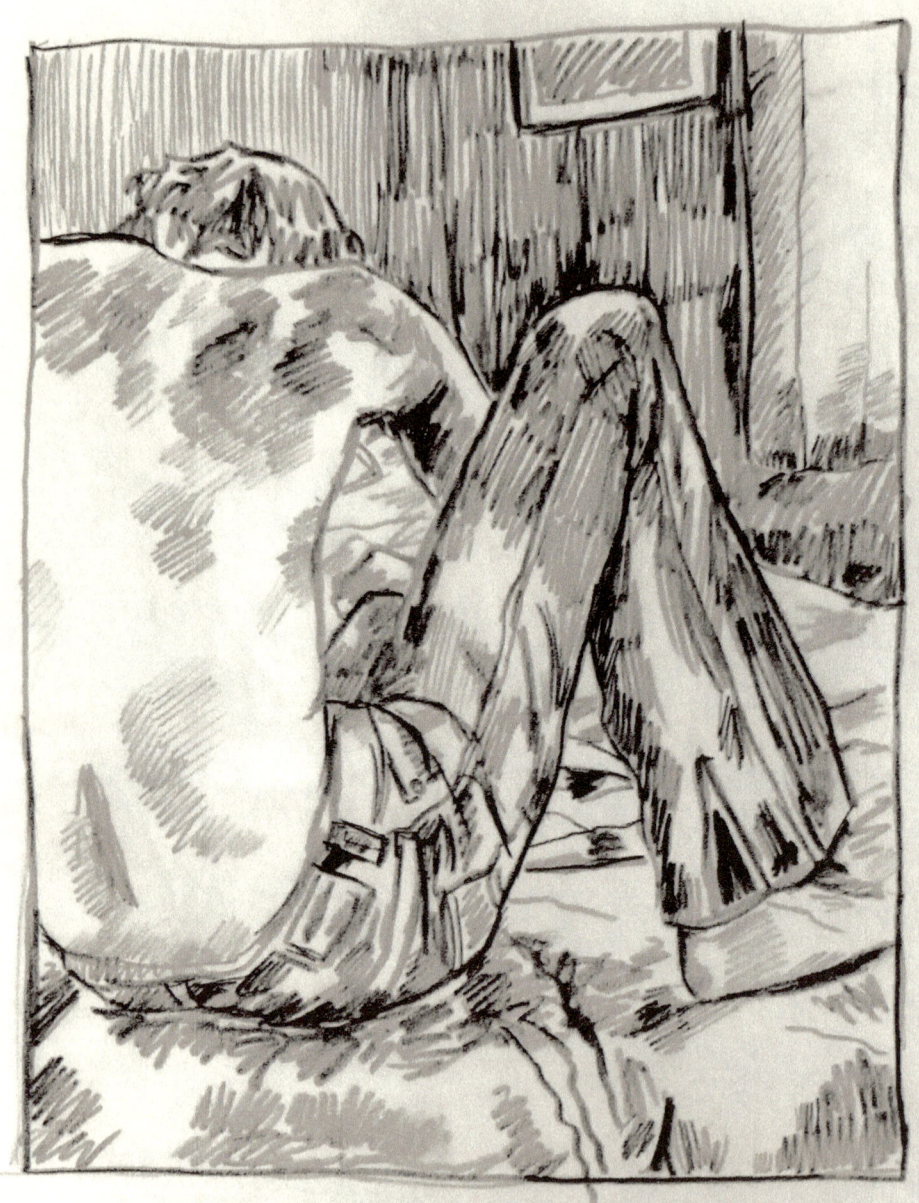

54

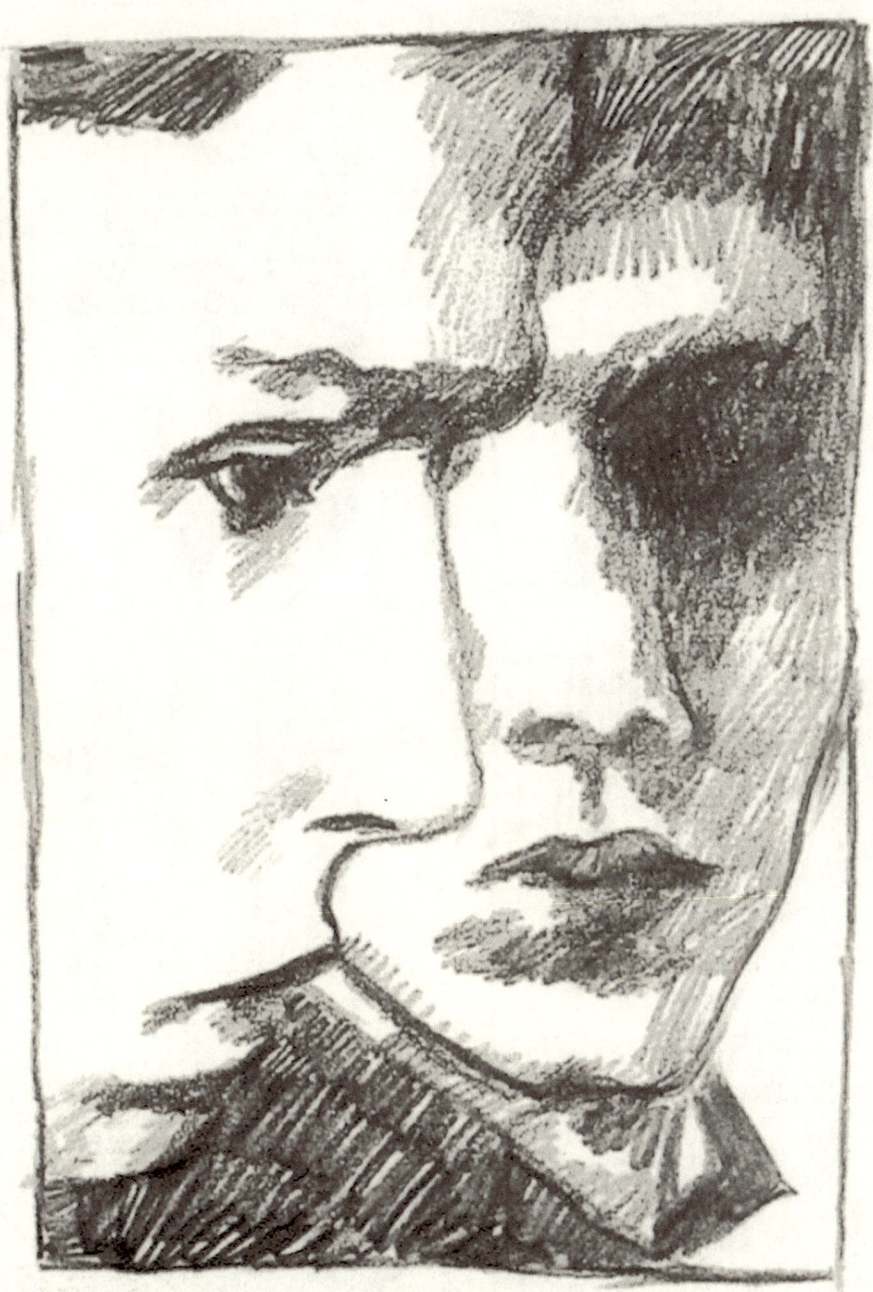

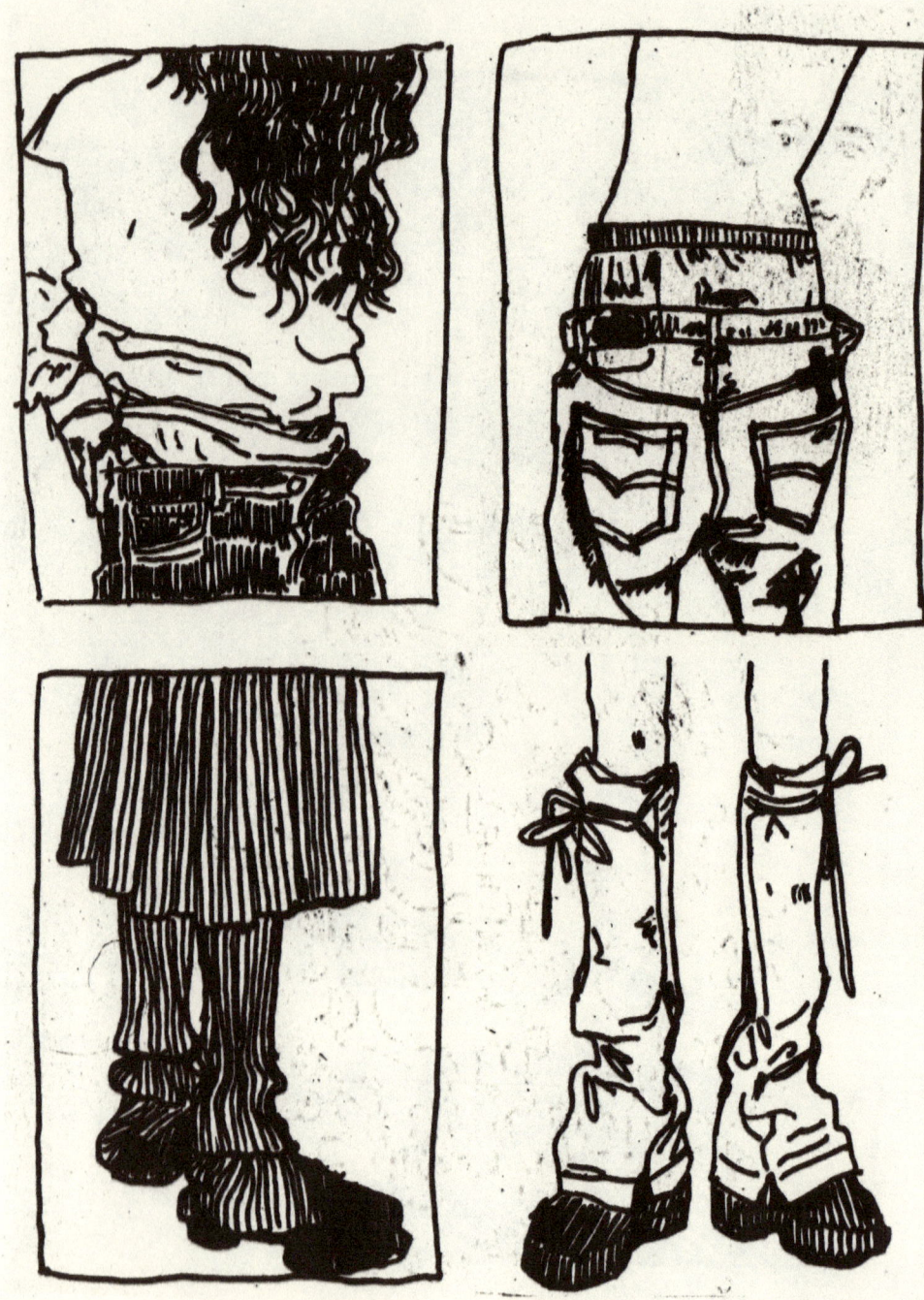

56

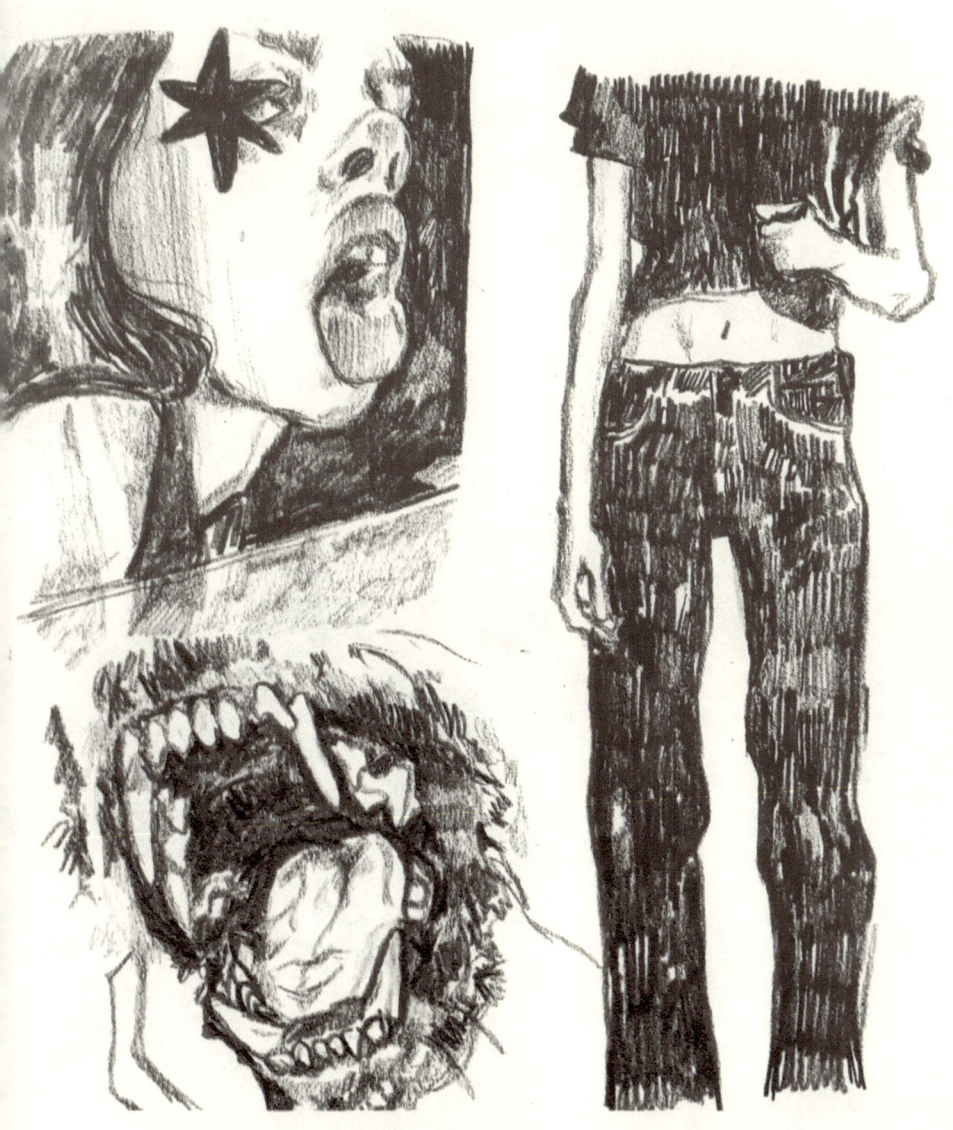

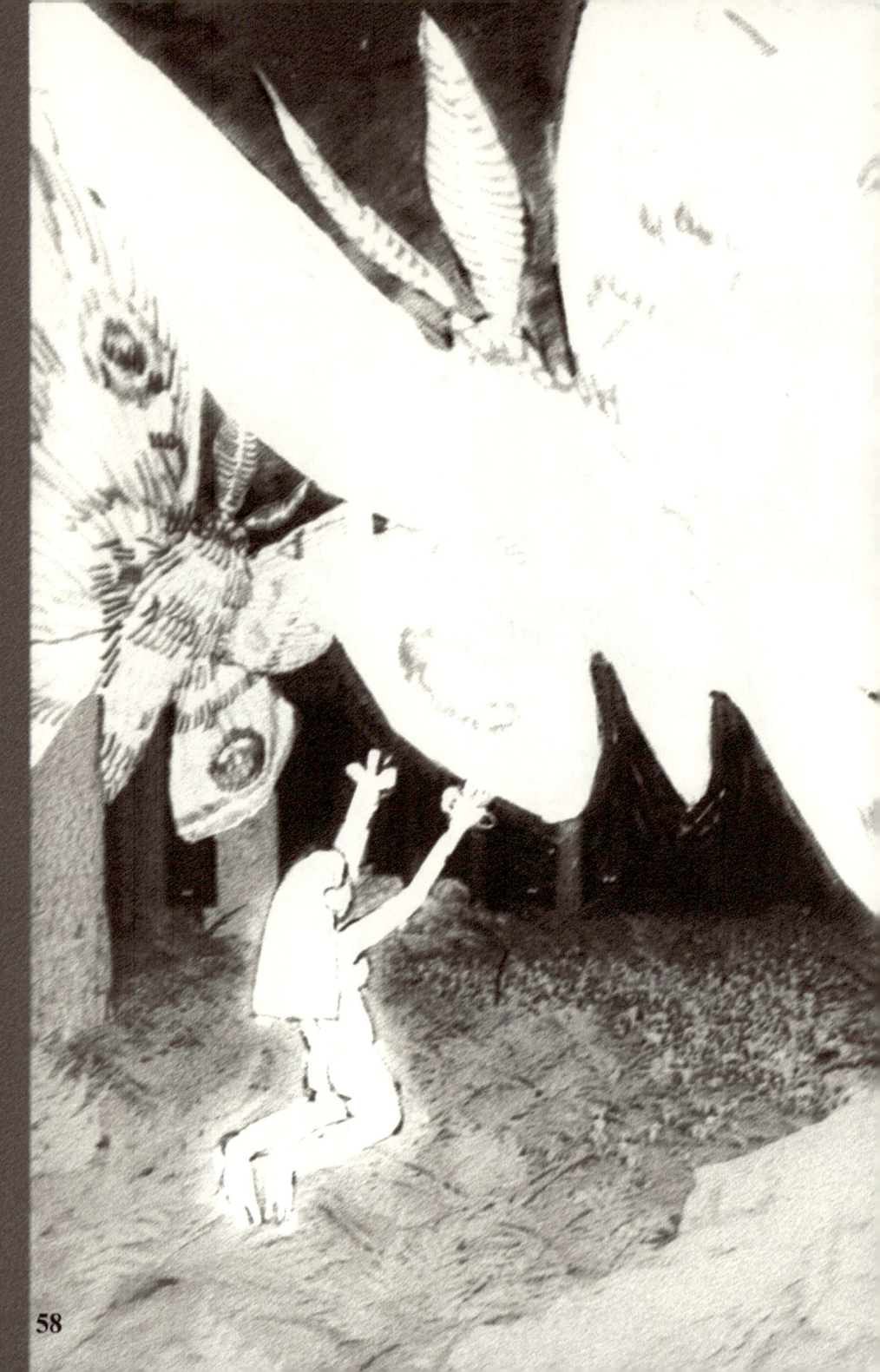

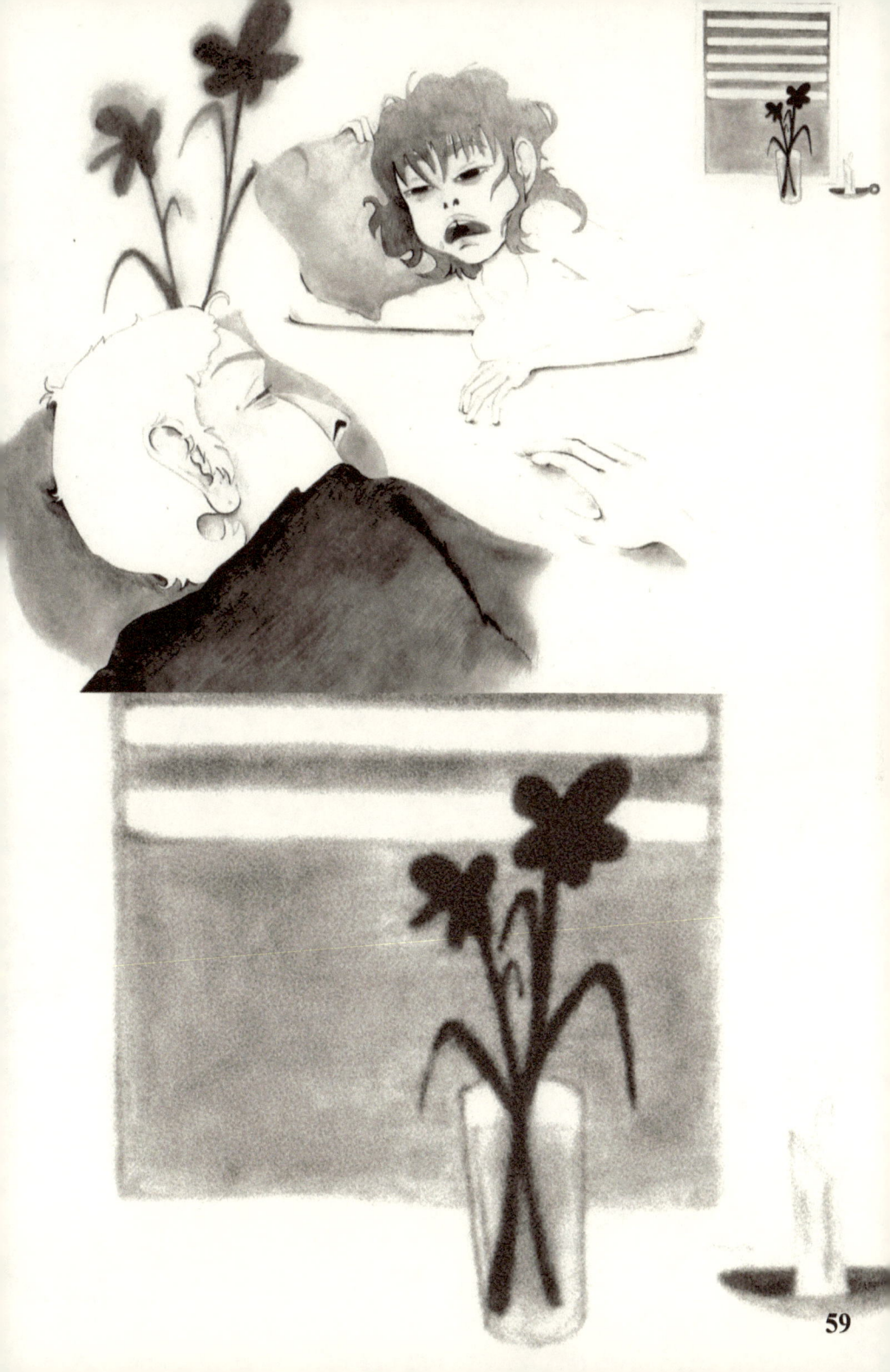

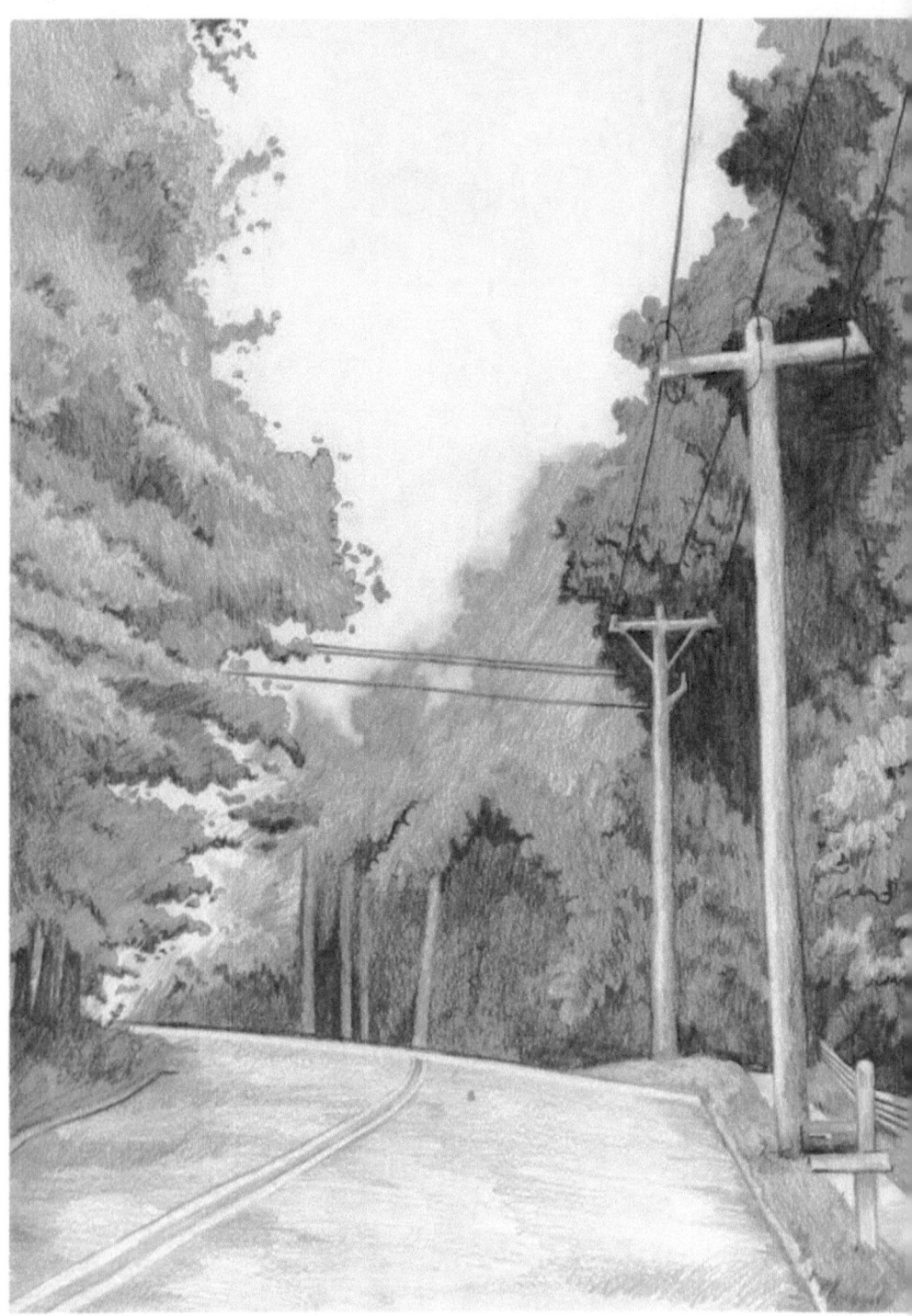

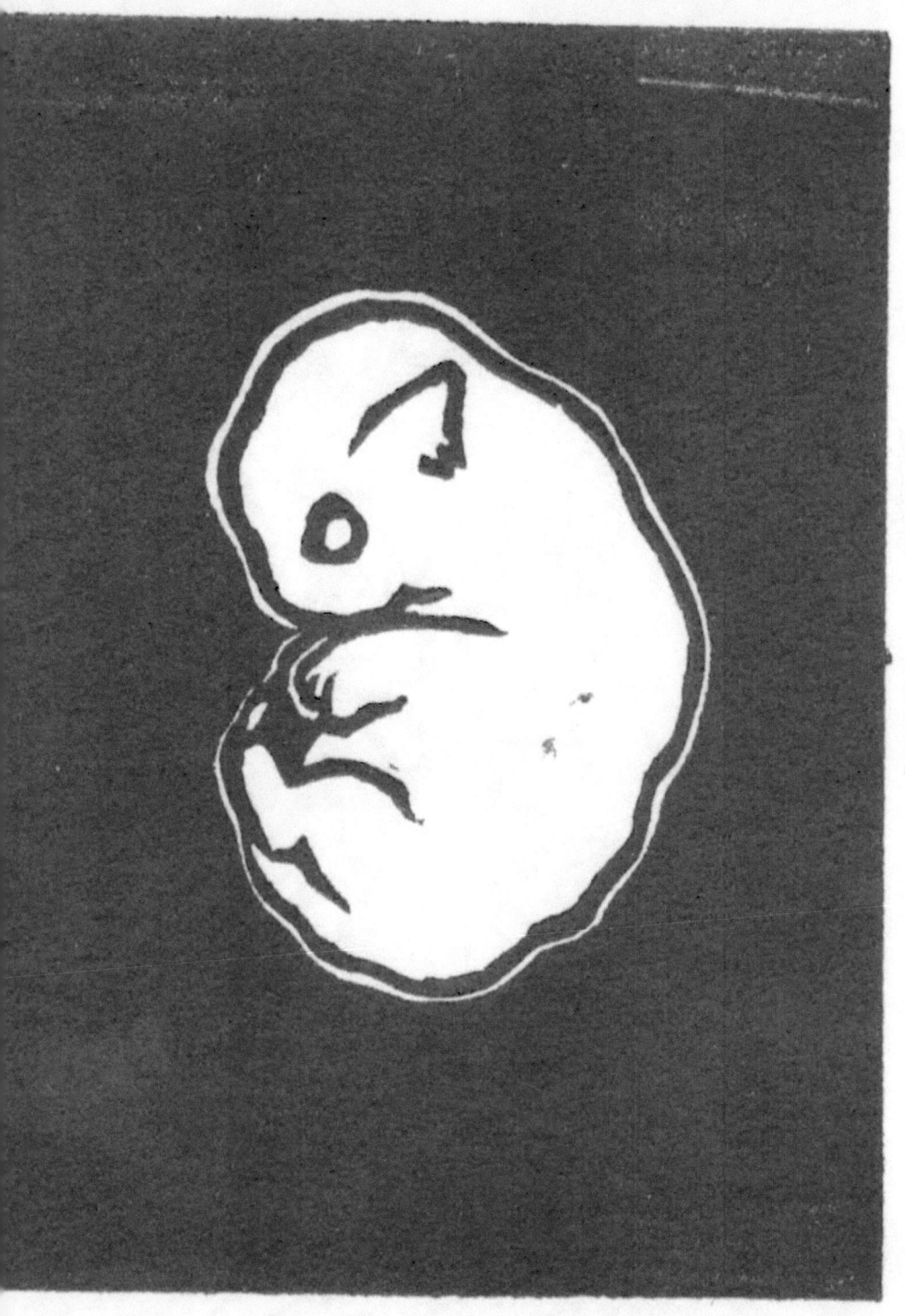

61

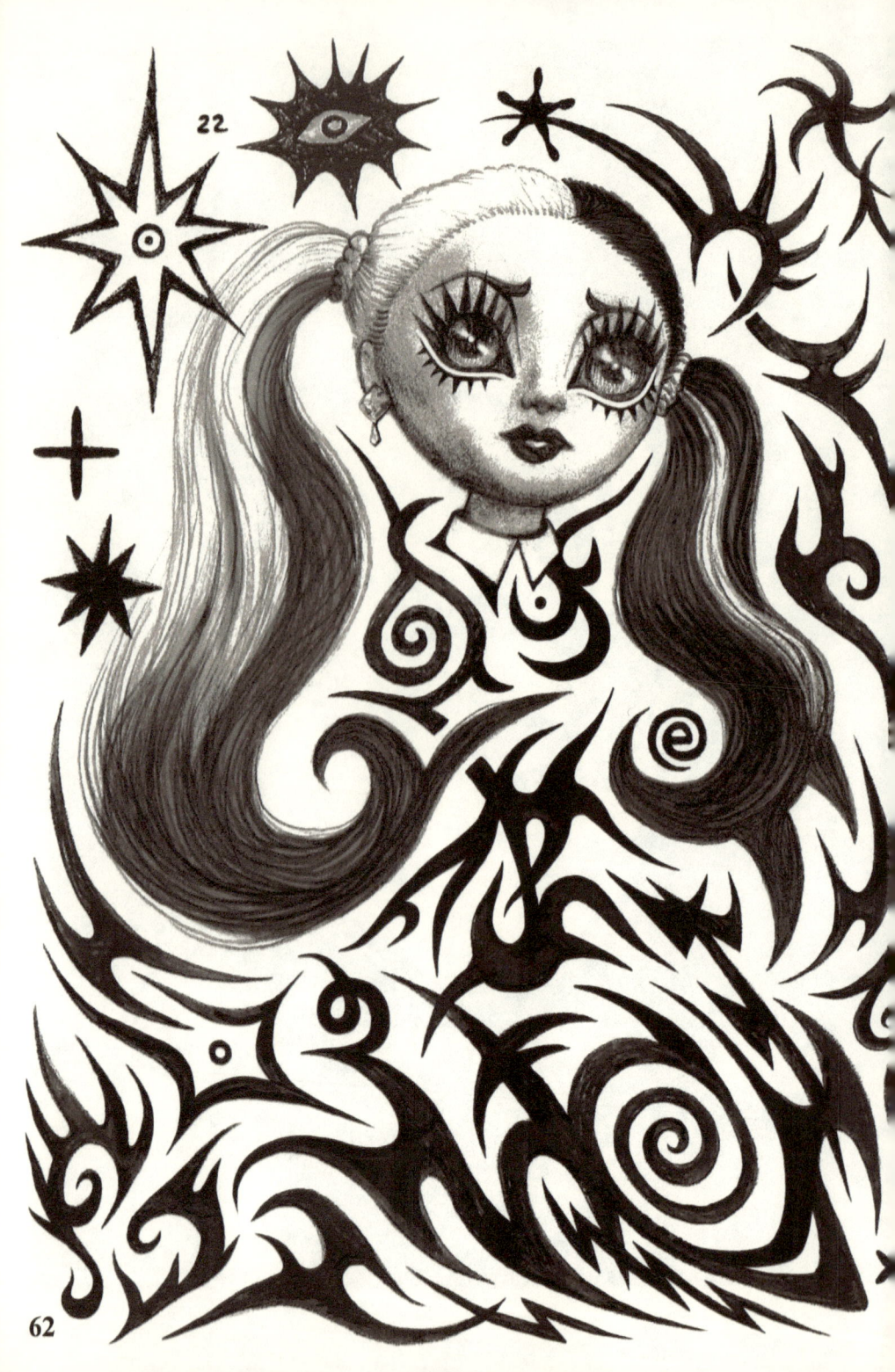

22

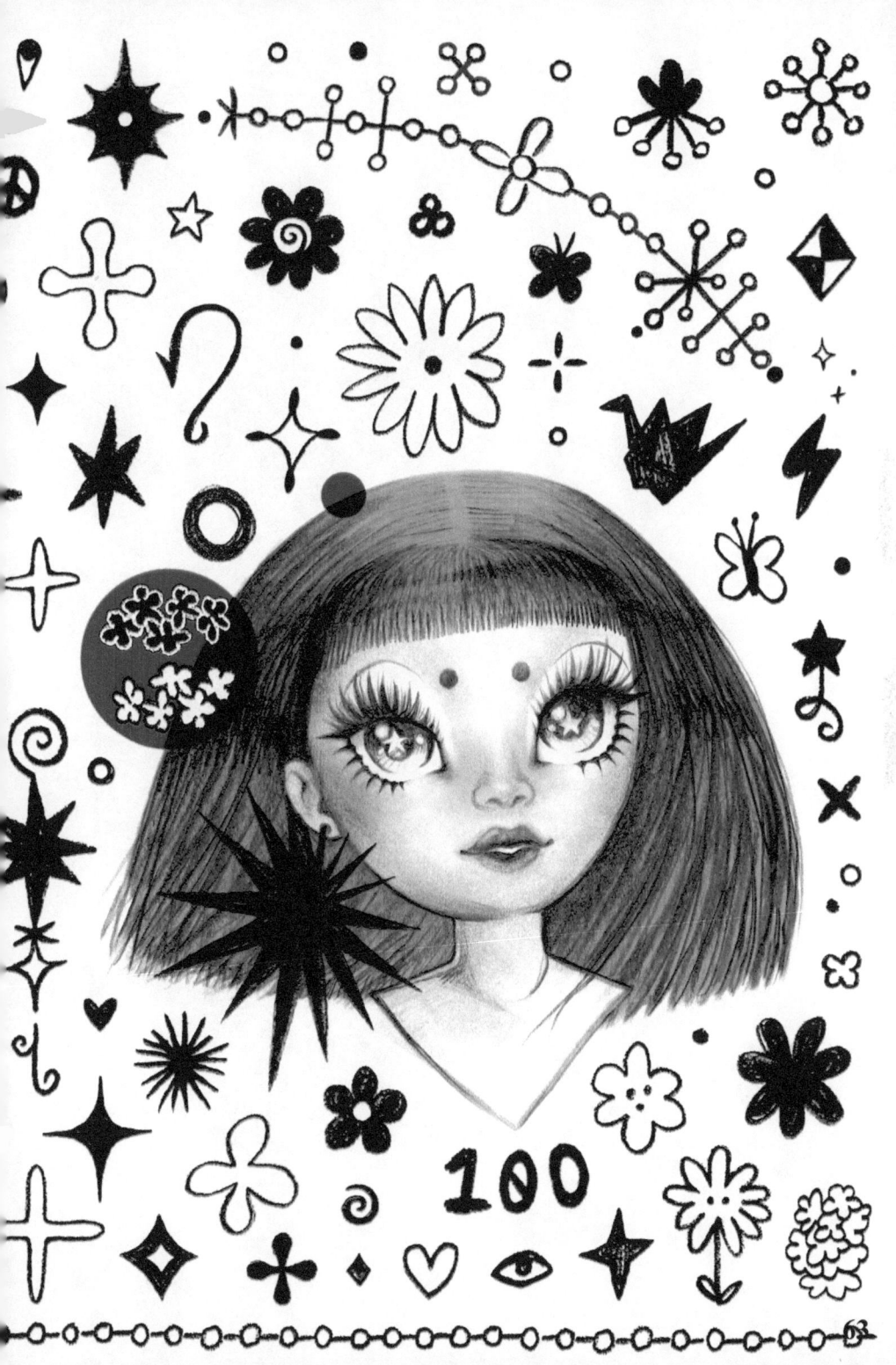

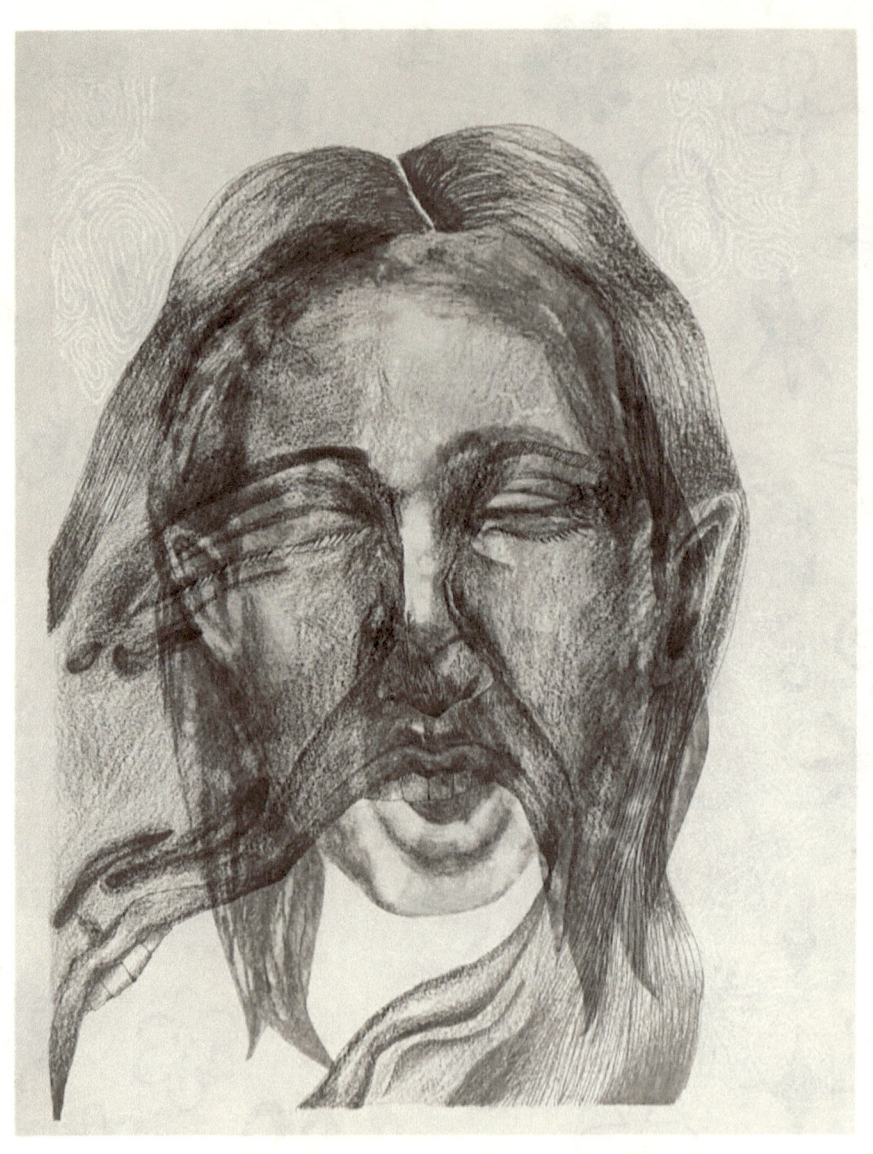

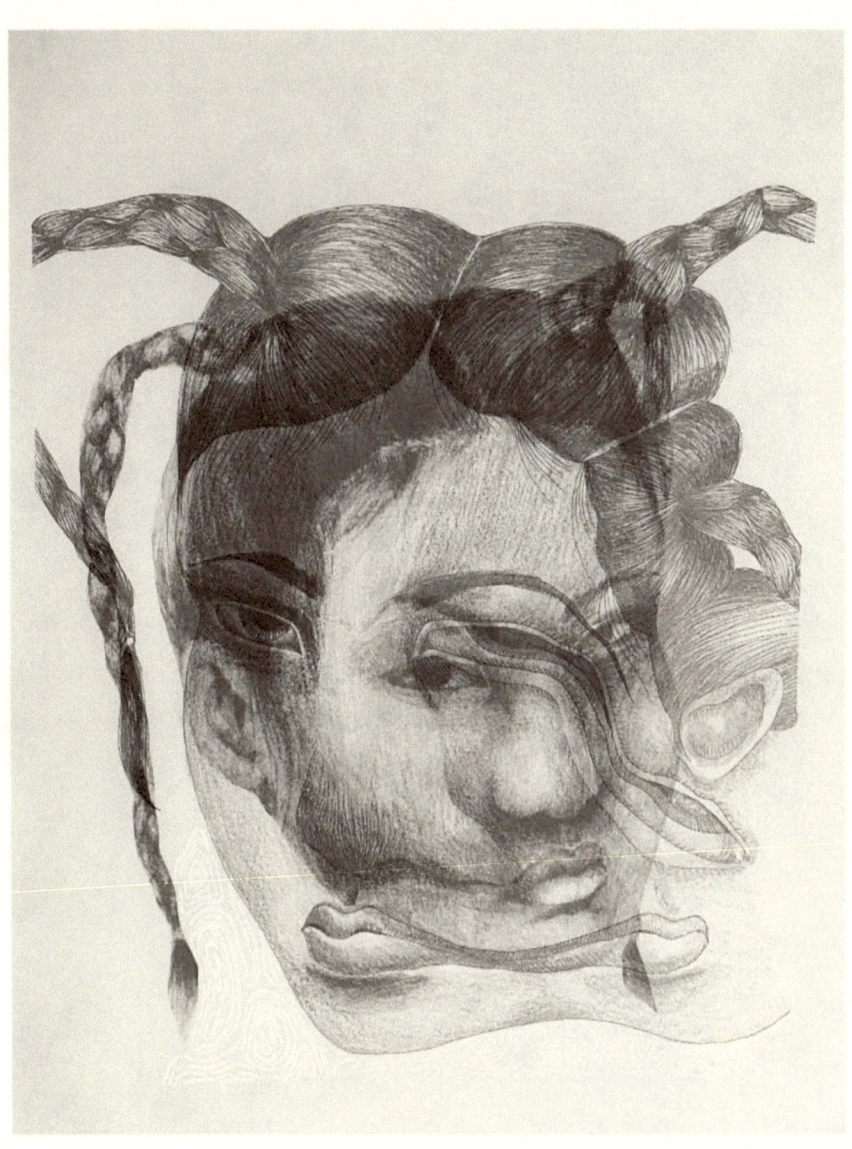

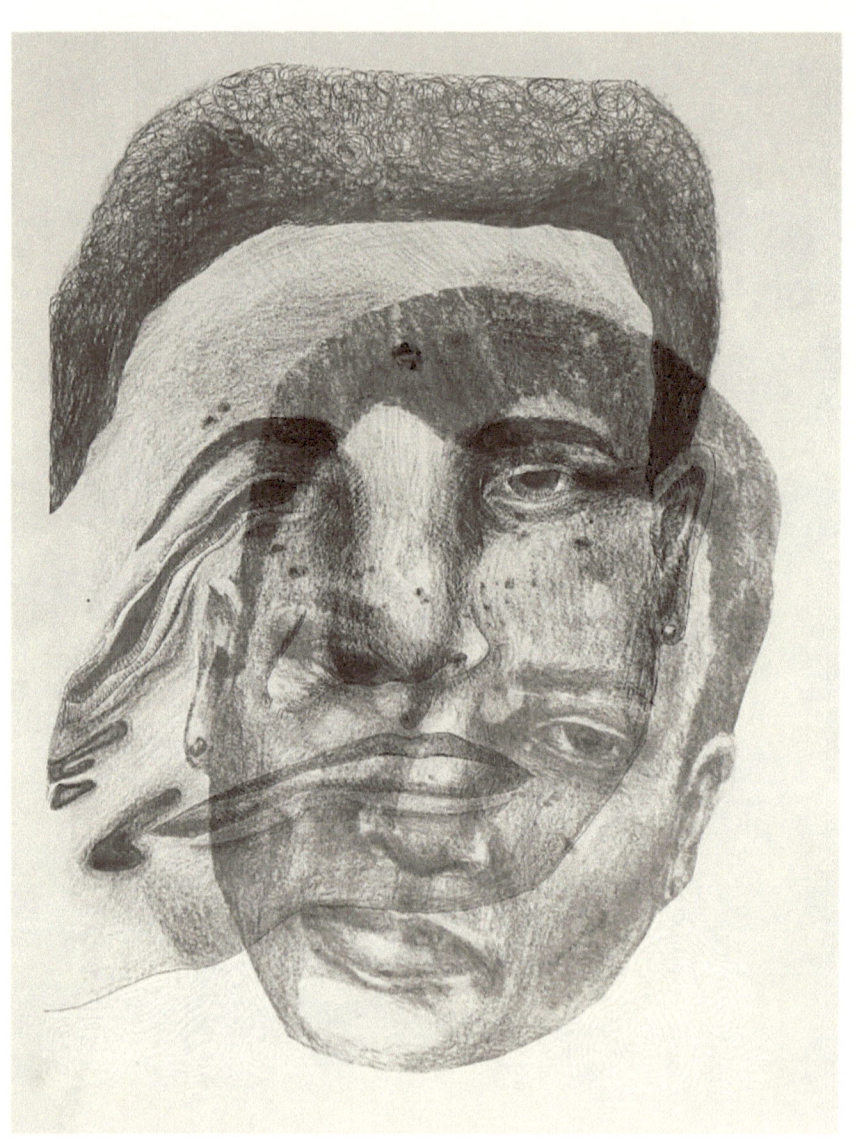

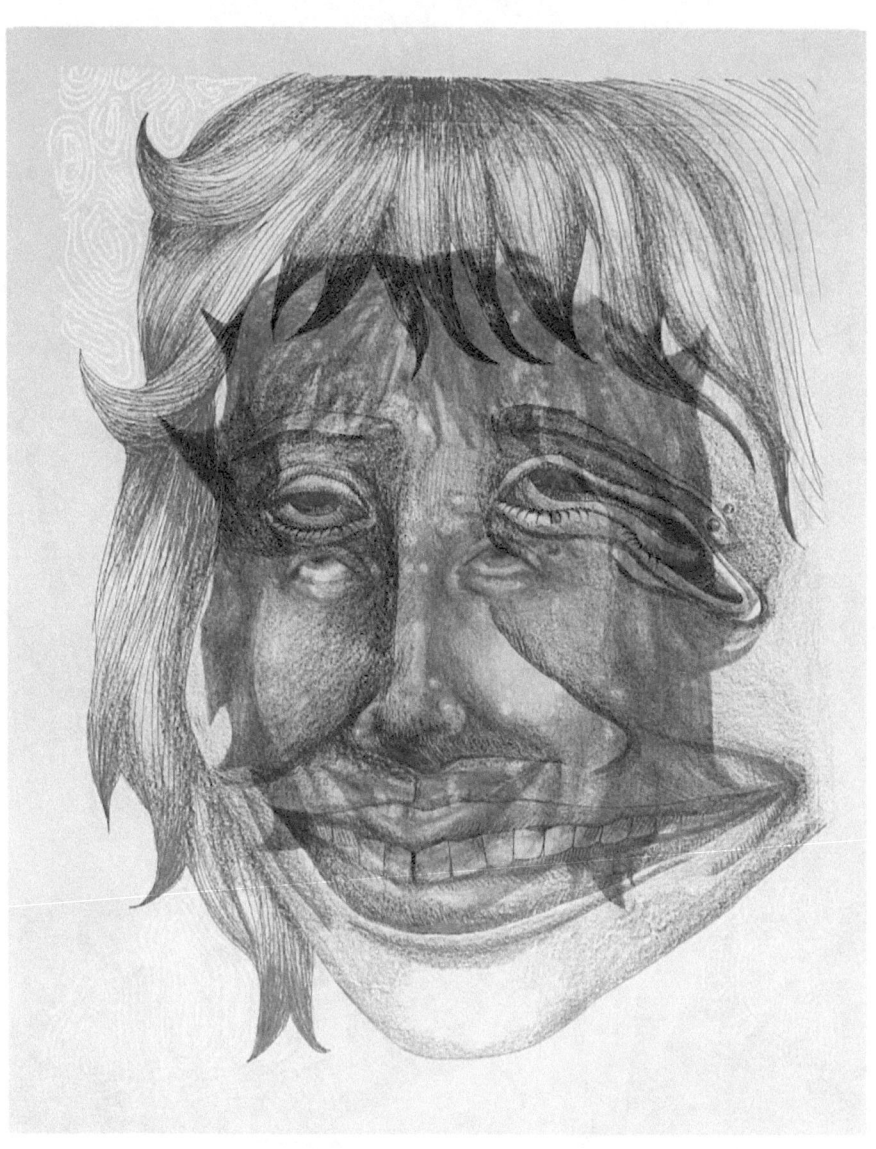

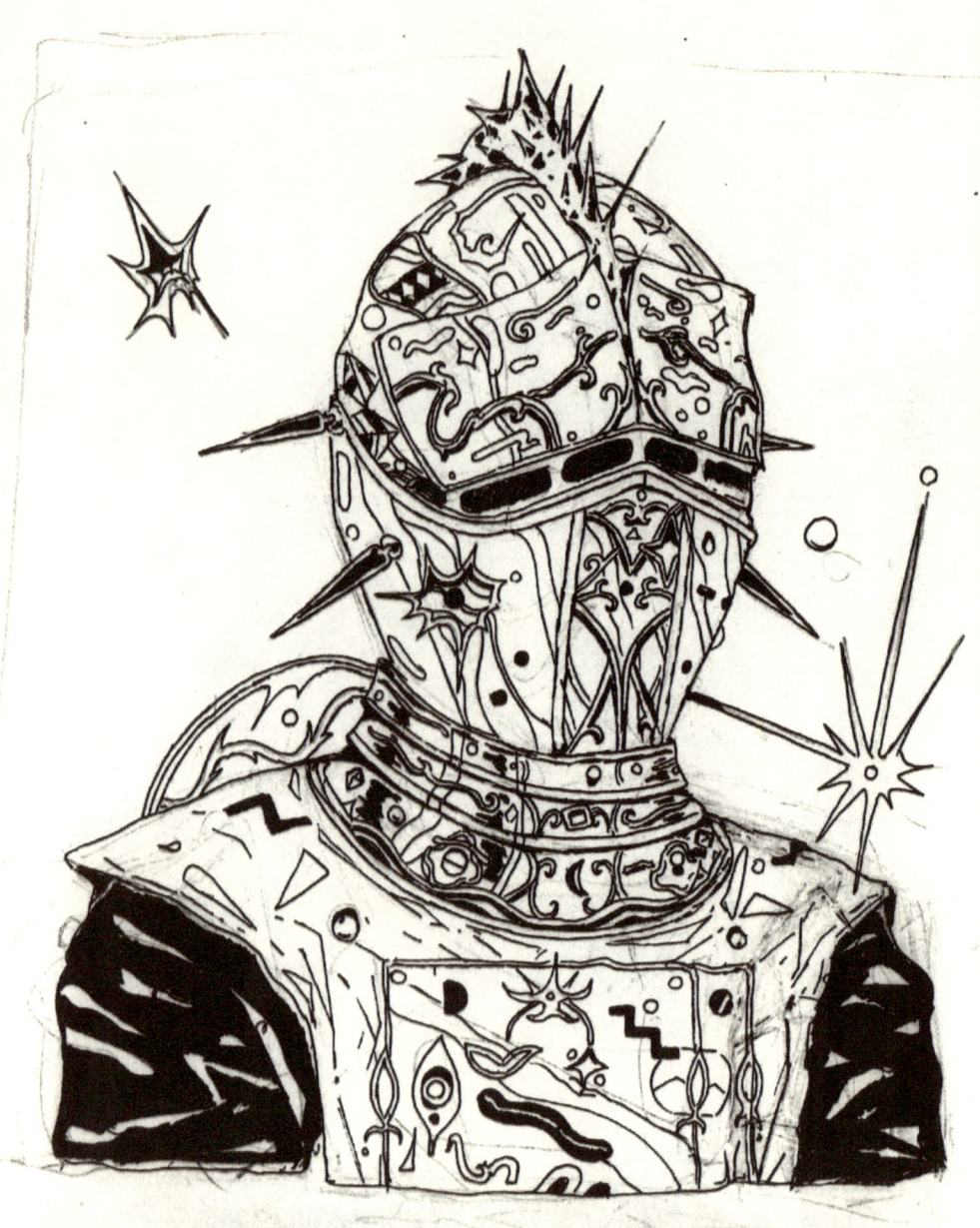

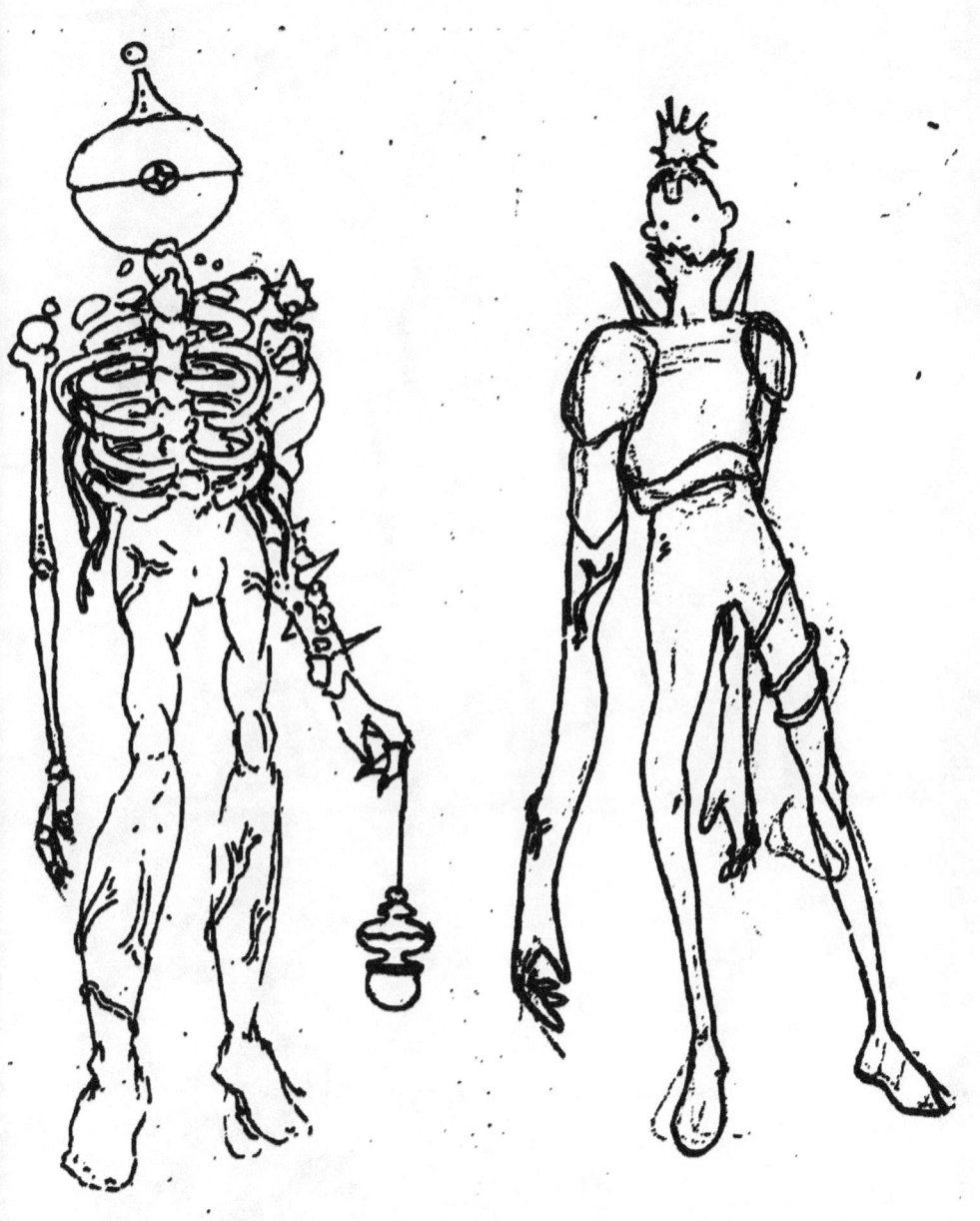

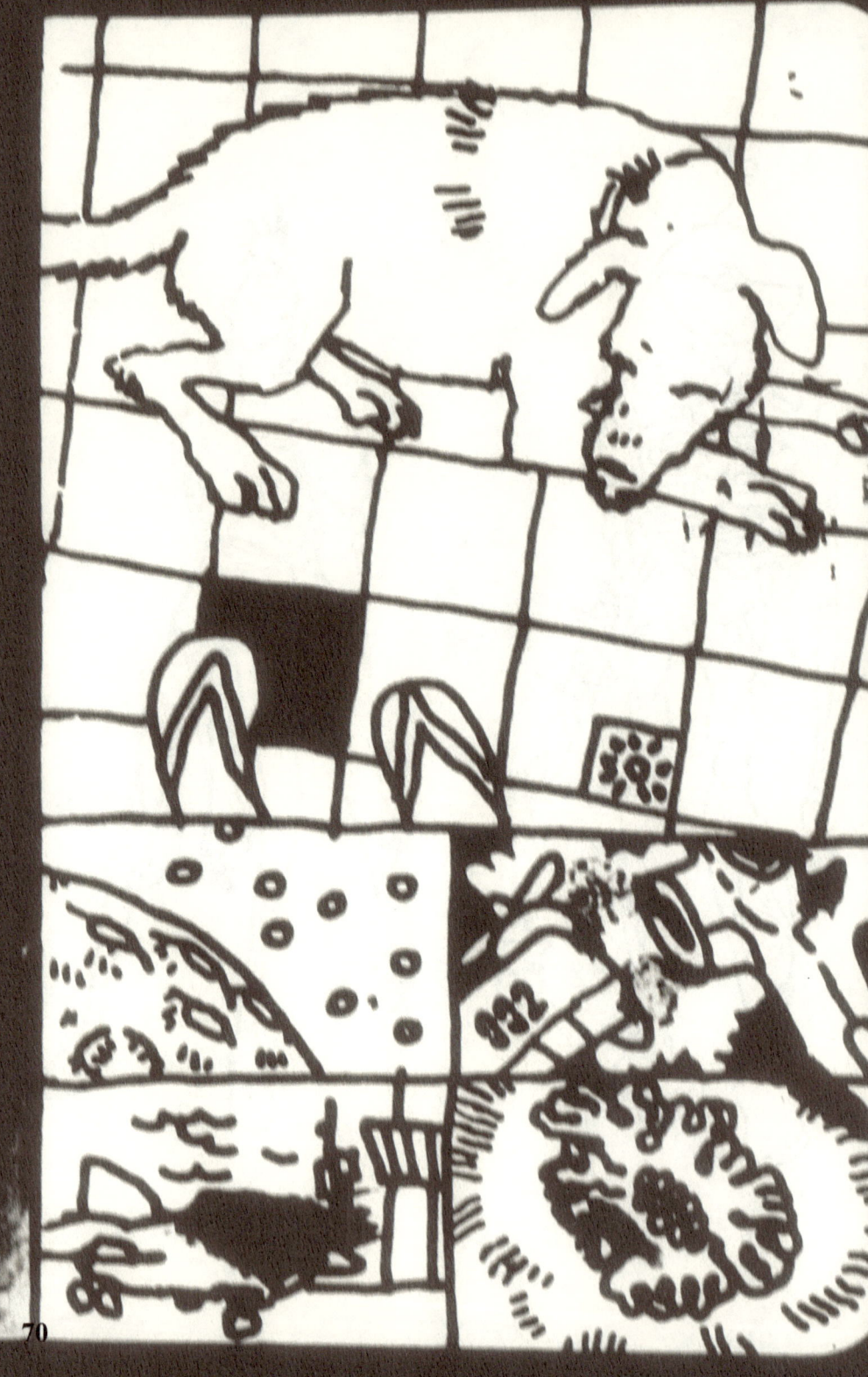

MOTHER

i DESPISE MY MOTHER i PiCK HER PURPLE FLOWERS
EVERYDAY SHE iS PATRONiSiNG AND CONTRADiCTiNG
i HOPE i AM NEVER LiKE HER i AM THE SPiTTiNG
iMAGE OF HER SHE iS MEAN AND CRUEL SHE iS
SOFT AND ~~GENT~~ GENTLE AND KiSSES MY HAND TWiCE
WHEN SHE THiNKS i'M ASLEEP WHEN i GROW UP
i WANT TO MOVE FAR AWAY FROM HER ALL i WANT iS
TO LiVE A BiKE RiDE AWAY FROM HER SHE SMELLS
LiKE WARM FOOD AND FRESH SALTWATER i NEED HER
i NEVER WANT TO BE NEAR HER AGAIN SHE CUTS ME
LiPSTiCK KiSSED APPLE SLiCES AND ON THE
WEEKEND SHE ~~~~ DiSLOCATED MY JAW AND
NO ONE KNEW NOT EVEN HER

mother

i despise my mother i pick her purple flowers
everyday she is patronising and contradicting
i hope am never like her i am the spitting
image of her she is mean and cruel she is
soft and gentle and kisses my hand twice
when she thinks i'm asleep when i grow up
i want to move far away from her all i want is
to live a bike ride away from her she smells
like warm food and fresh saltwater i need her
i never want to be near her again she cuts me
lipstick kissed apple slices and on the
weekend she dislocated my jaw and
no one knew not even her

BANANA GRAMS

BEEN
CALLED
DIG
PEN
CLIT
SICKLE
ROT
LEAK
PINCH
CUT
CUT
CUT
CUT
BAD

bananagrams

been
called
dig
pen
clit
sickle
rot
leak
pinch
cut
cut
cut
cut
72 bad

i TAKE THE LONG WAY HOME SO THAT THE
MAGPIES WON'T BITE.

i MISS MY MOTHER AND MY GRIMY LAMP. i WAKE UP
'N PLASTIC SHEETS, COLD AND SORE LIKE
A DOG'S BITE. i ACHE iN PLACES HE'LL NEVER
KNOW. iNSTEAD, i TALK LEFTIST AND ANTi CAPiTALiST TO HiM.
i WRITE HALF A POEM WHEN i GET HOME.
IKE A BAD iMiTATiON OF SYLViA PLATH, iT GOES:

"i ACHE FOR YOU BAD. PARTS OF ME HEAVE AND
PUSH FOR YOU. WHEN i THiNK ABOUT YOU,
i CAN HARDLY BREATHE. iT'S NOT FAiR.

HERE i AM, ALL OF ME. THiS iS ME, i PRESENT.

ALL OF ME ACHES."

sylvia plath

i take the long way home so that the
magpies won't bite.
i miss my mother and my grimy lamp. i wake up
on plastic sheets, cold and sore like
a dog's bite. i ache in places he'll never
know. instead, i talk leftist and anti capitalist to him.
i write half a poem when i get home.
like a bad imitation of sylvia plath, it goes:
"i ache for you bad. parts of me heave and
push for you. when i think about you
i can hardly breathe. it's not fair.
here i am, all of me. this is me, i present.
all of me aches."

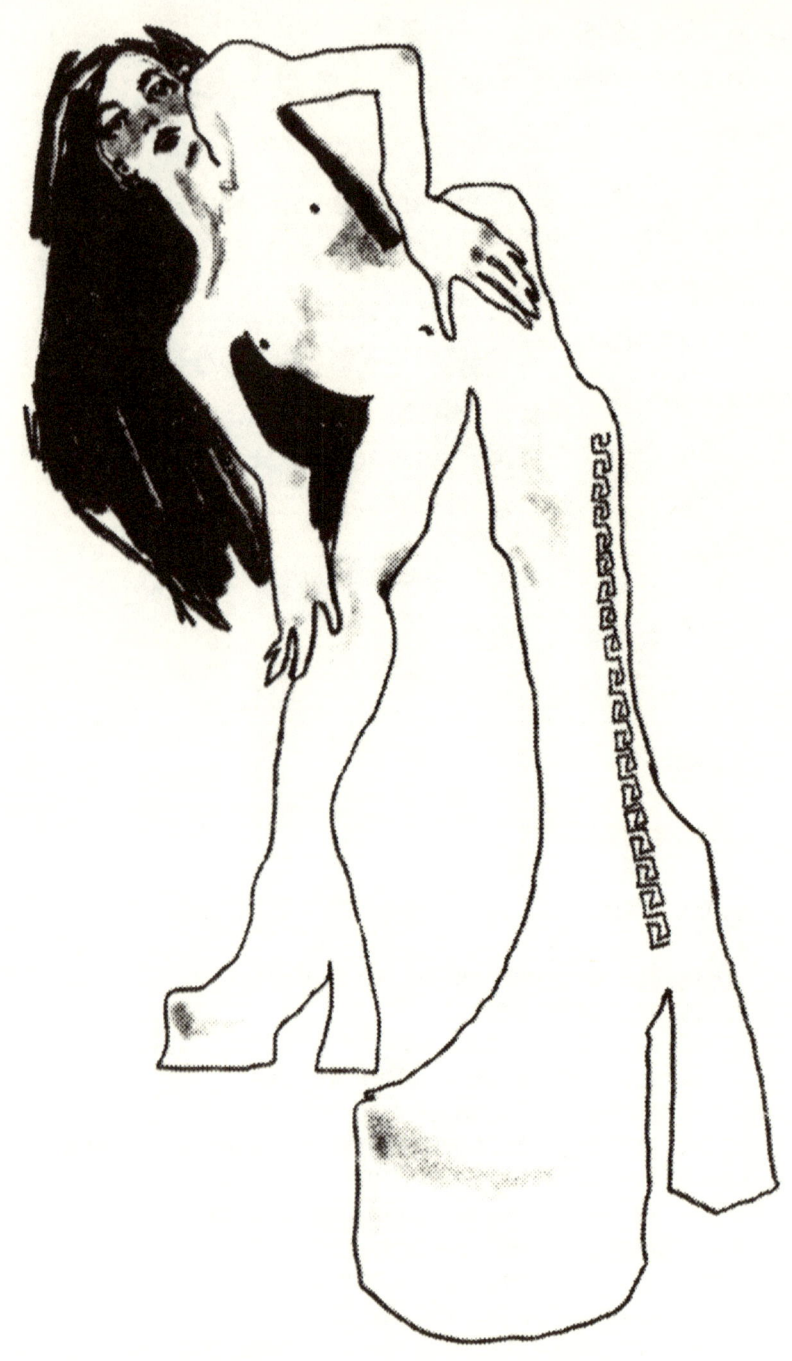

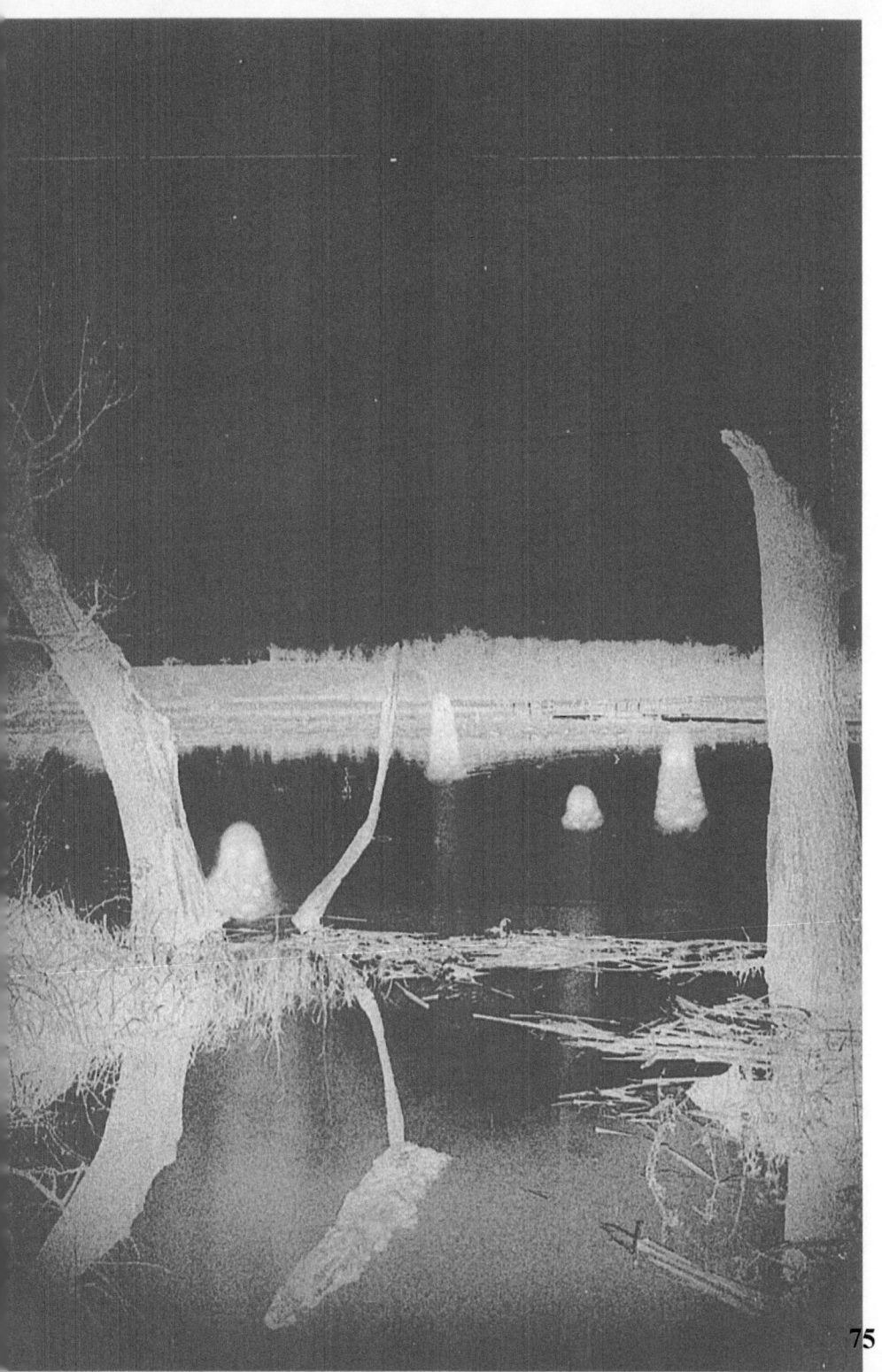

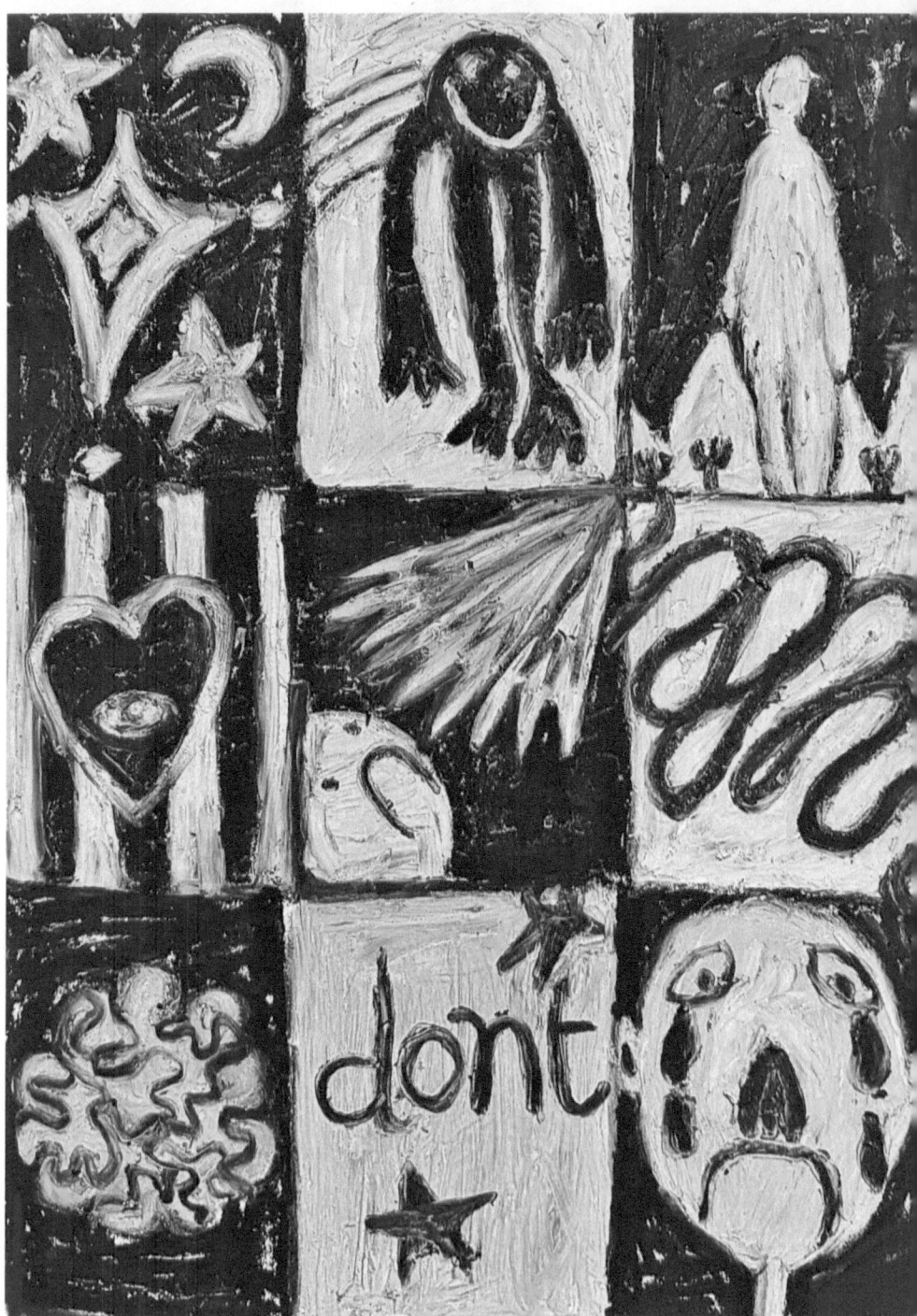

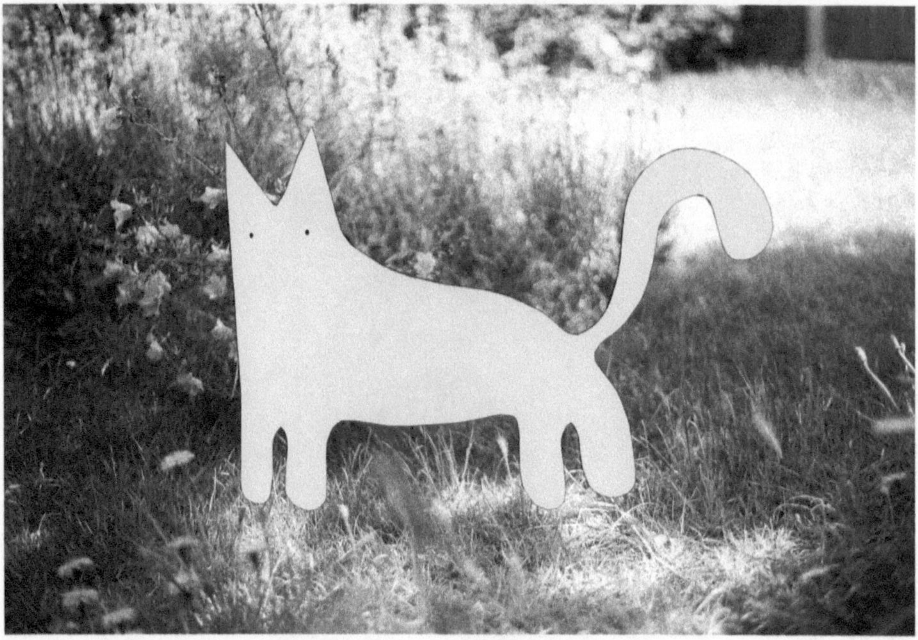

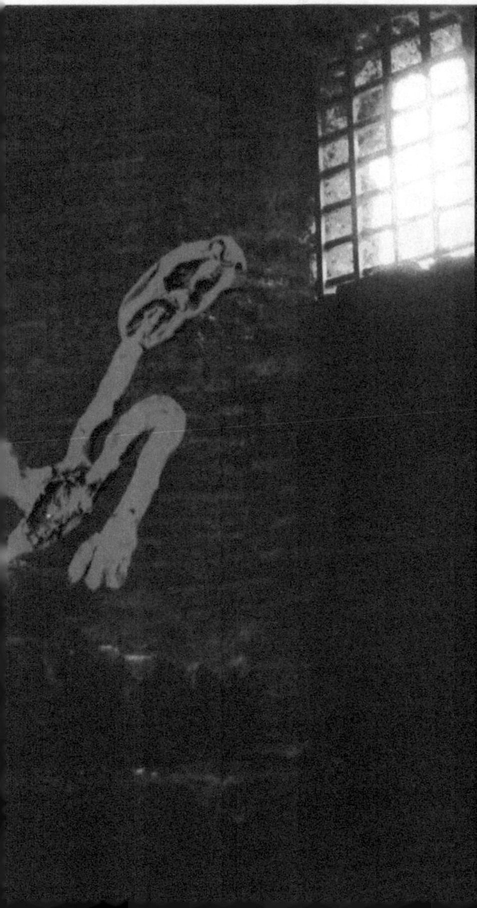

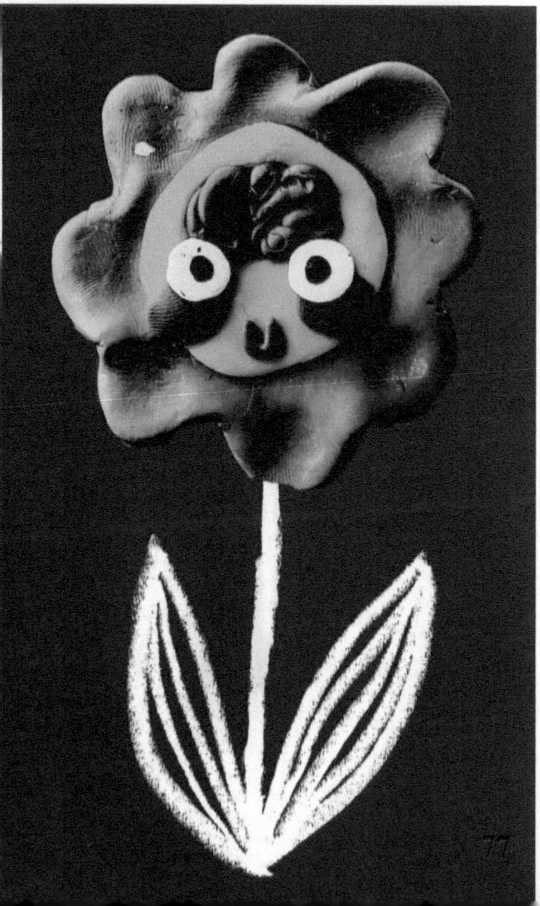

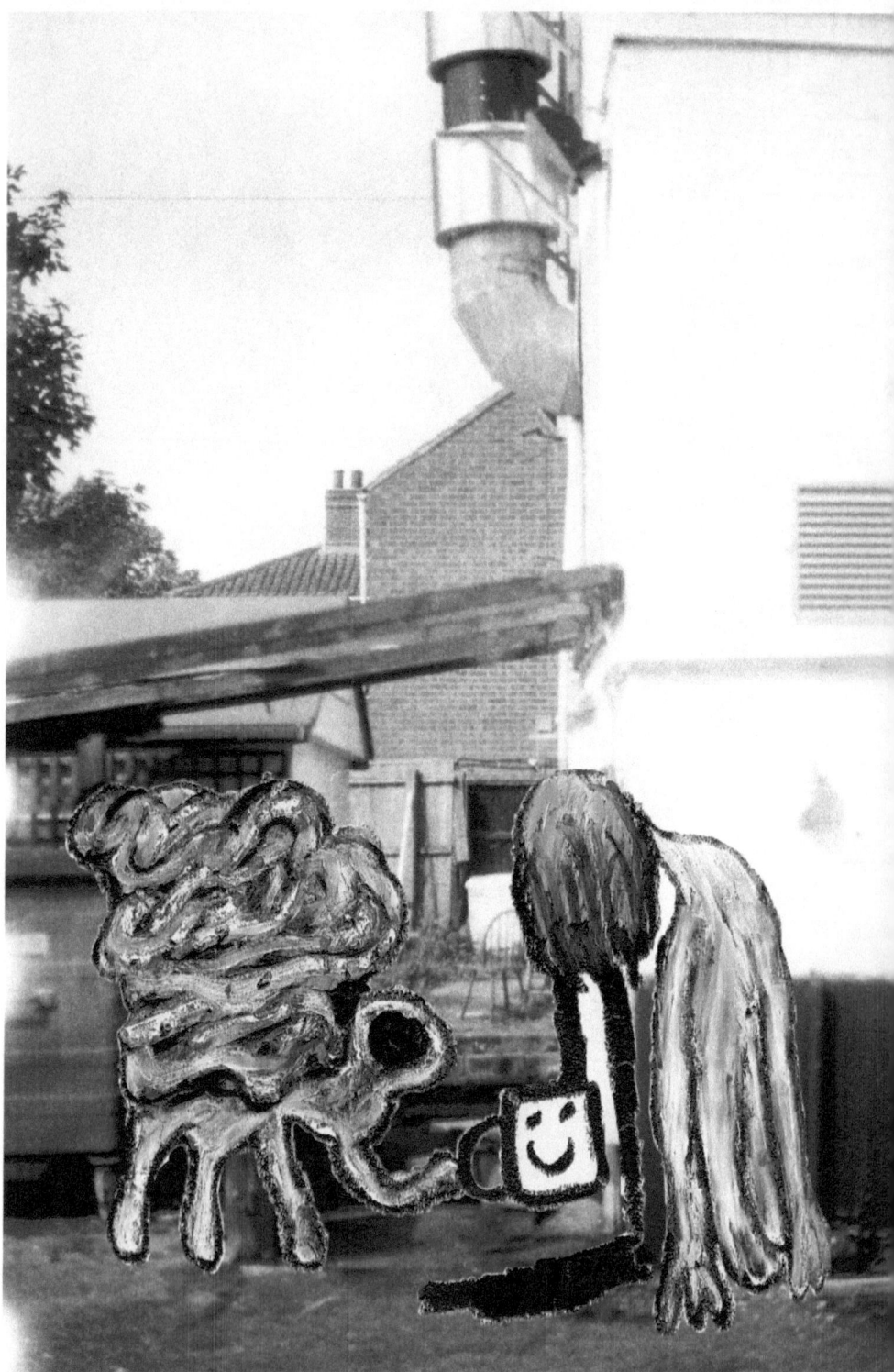

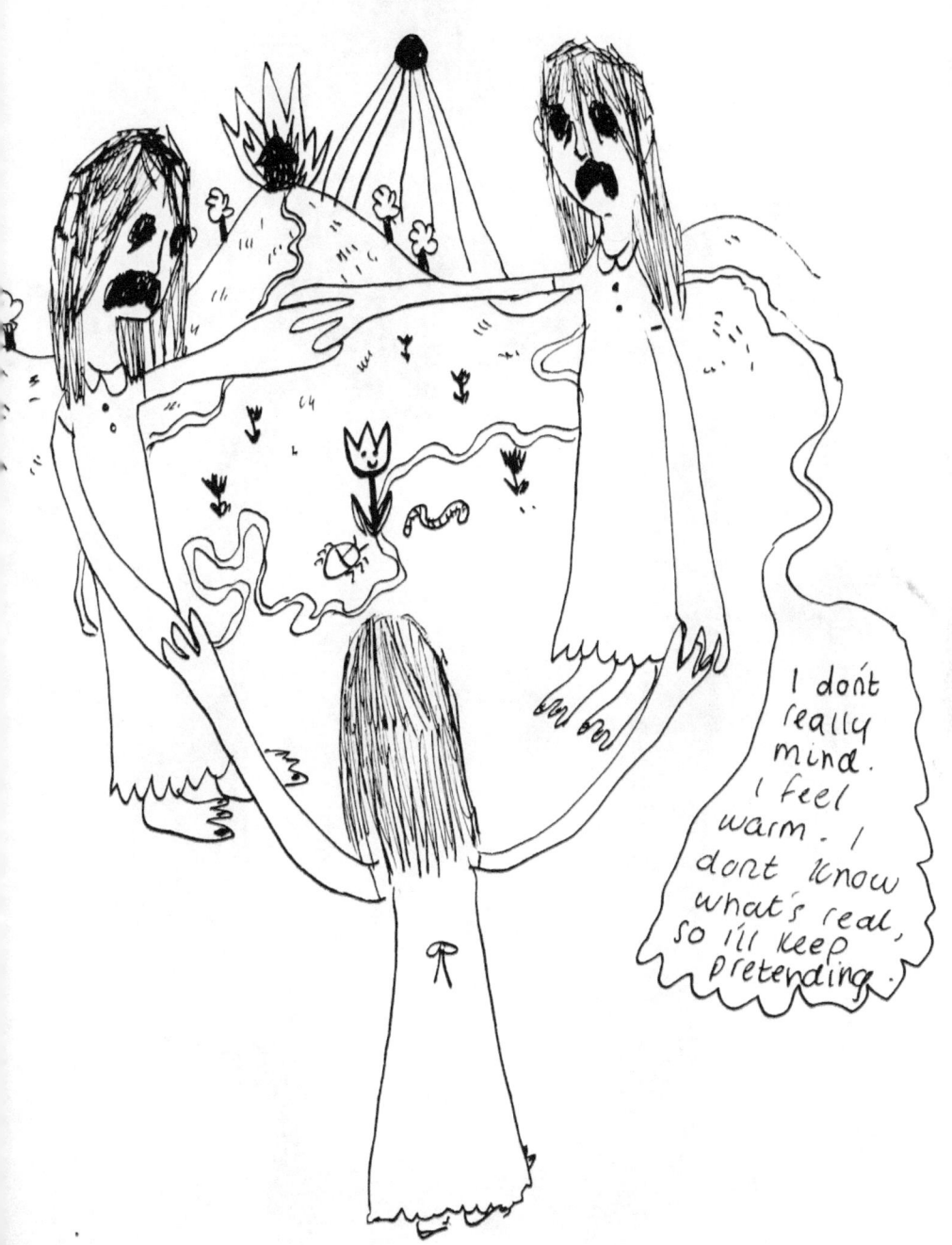

I don't really mind. I feel warm. I don't know what's real, so I'll keep pretending.

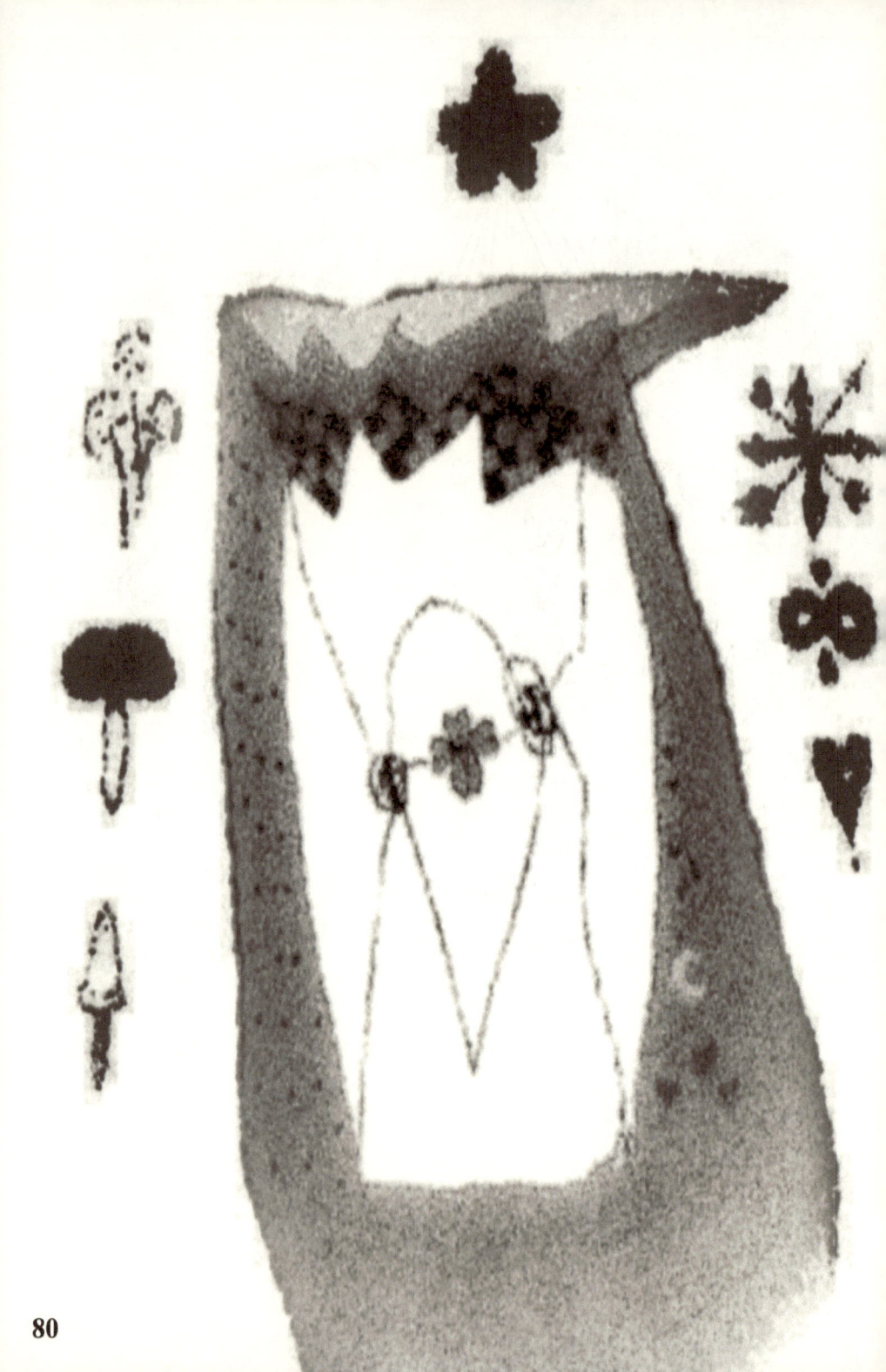

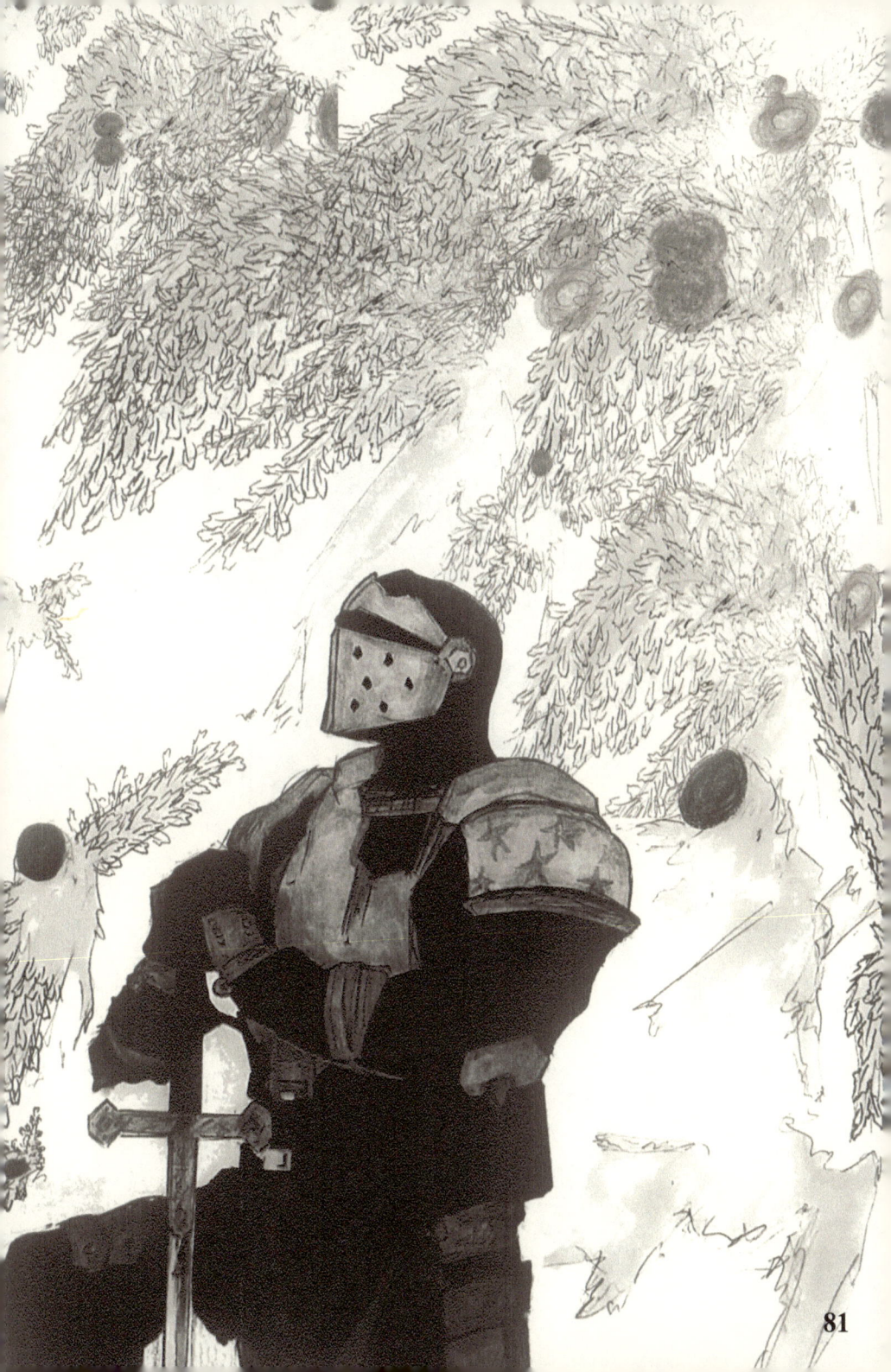

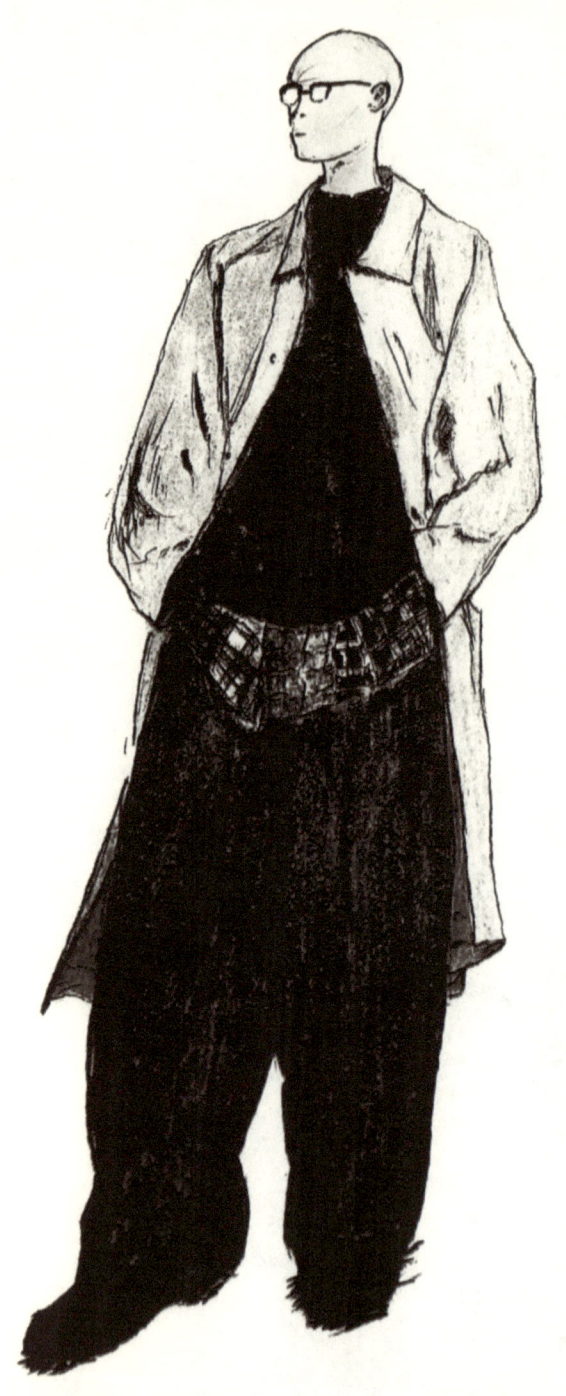

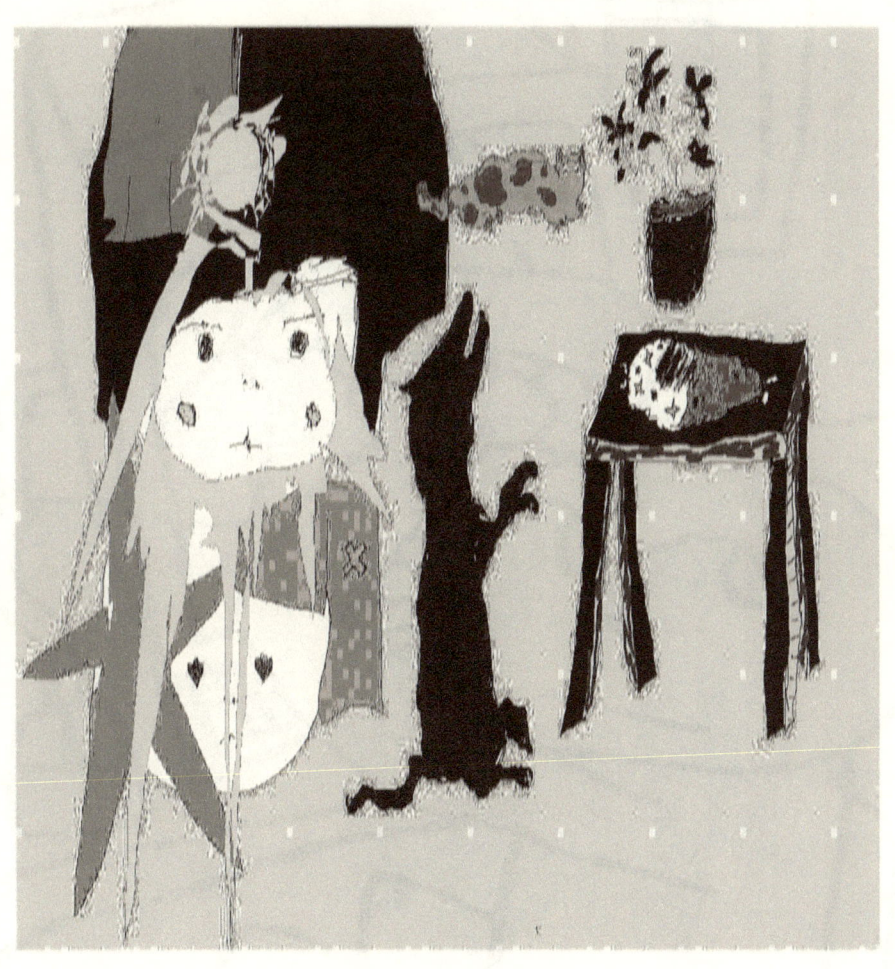

83

84

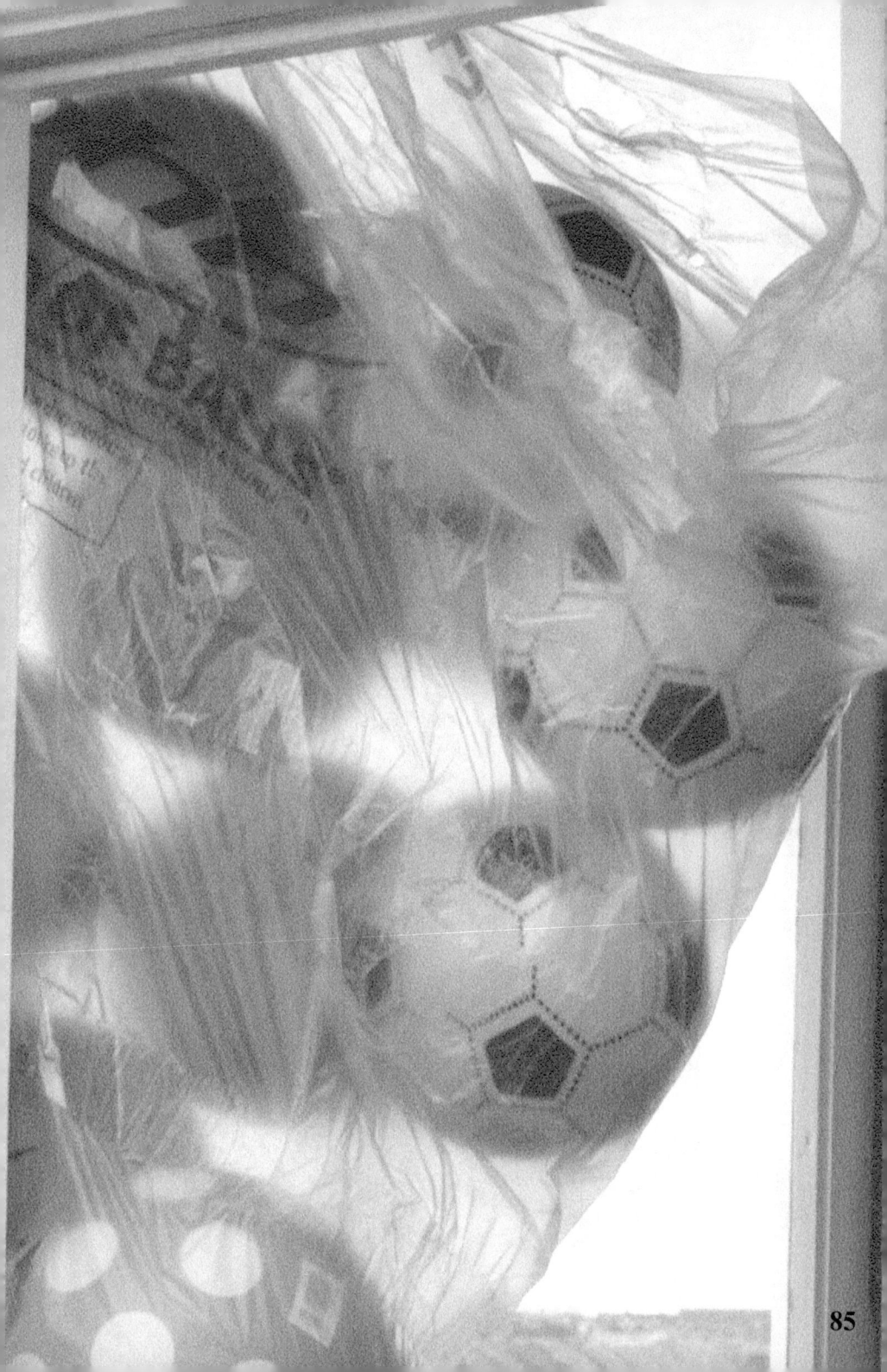

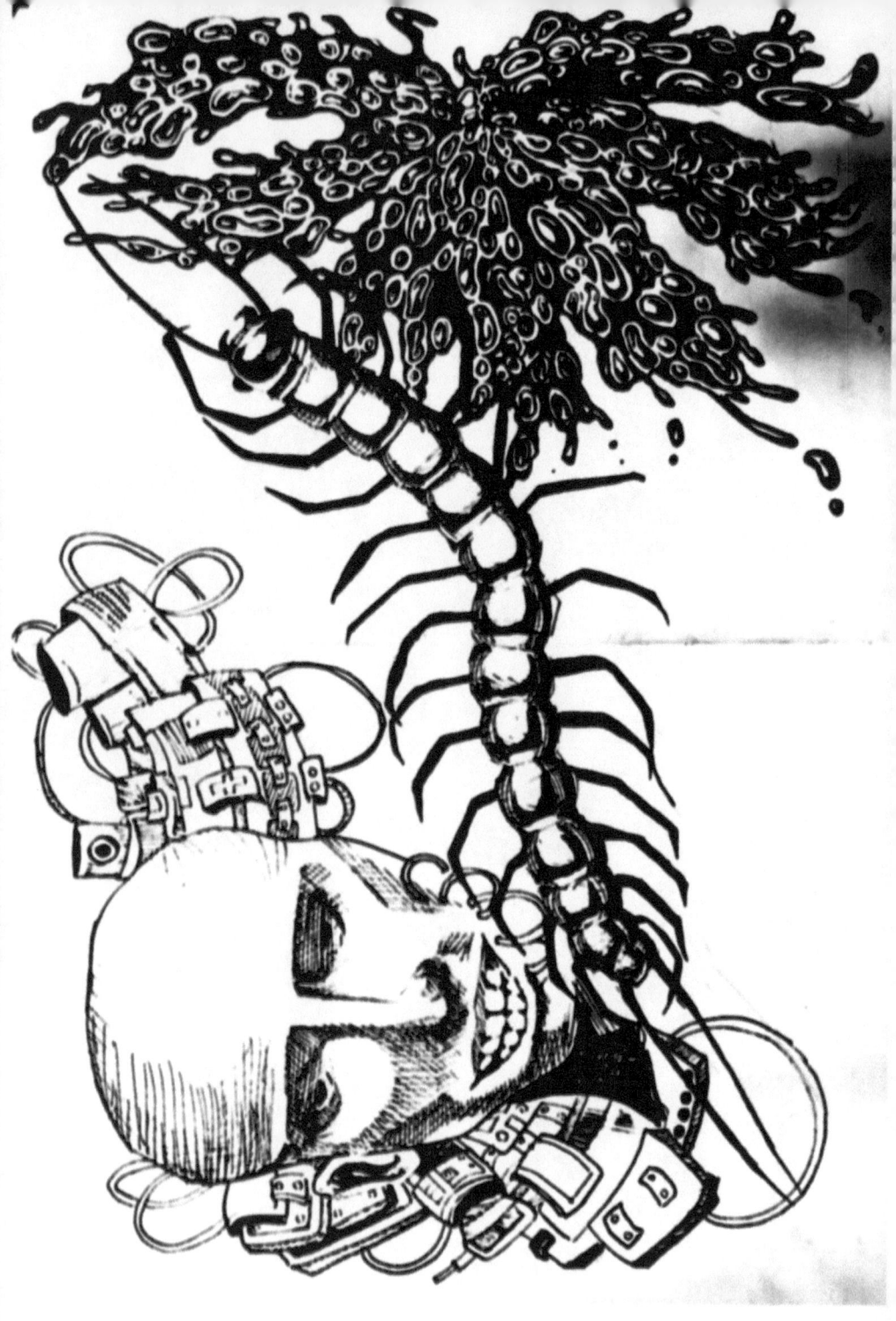

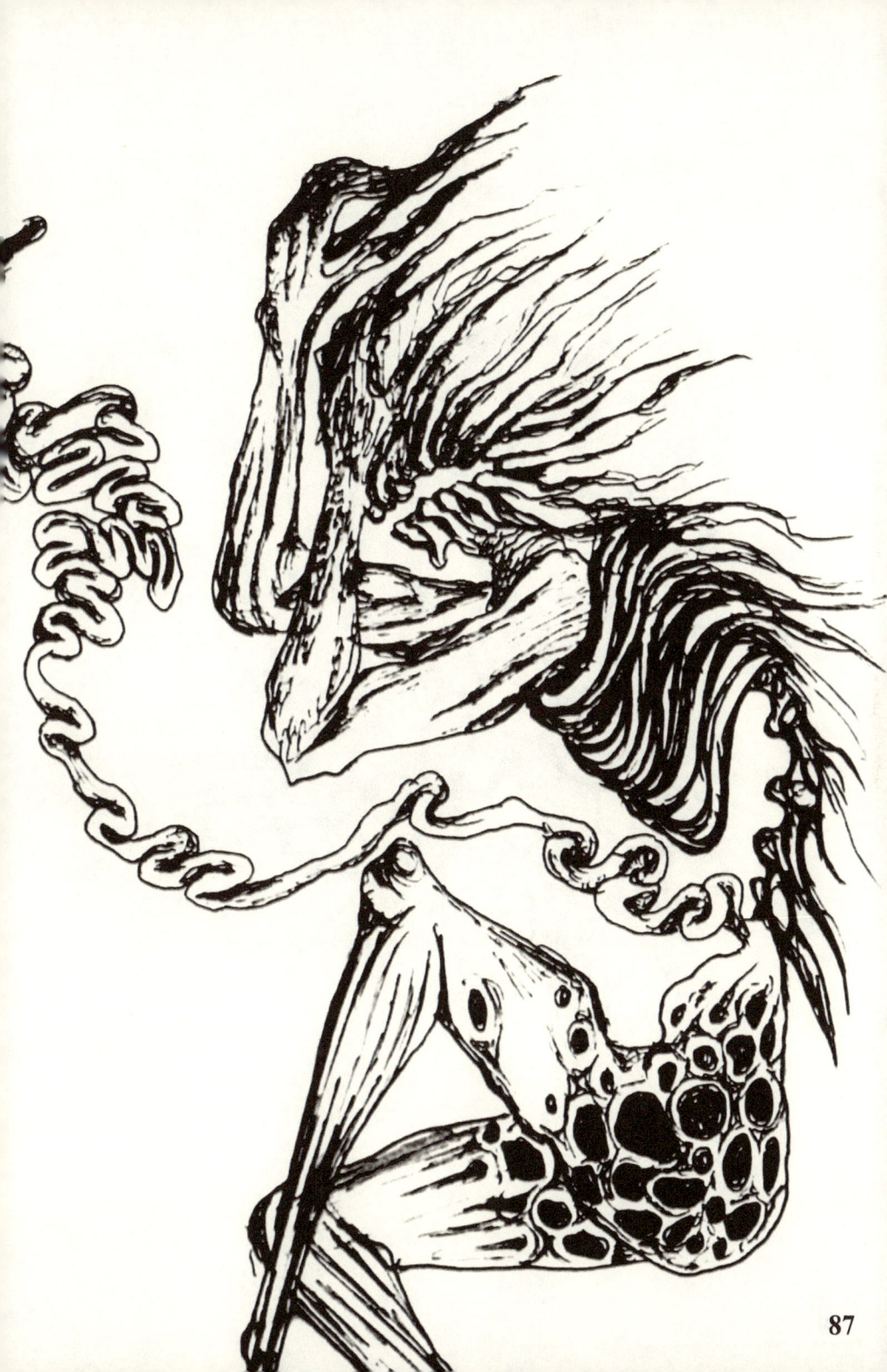

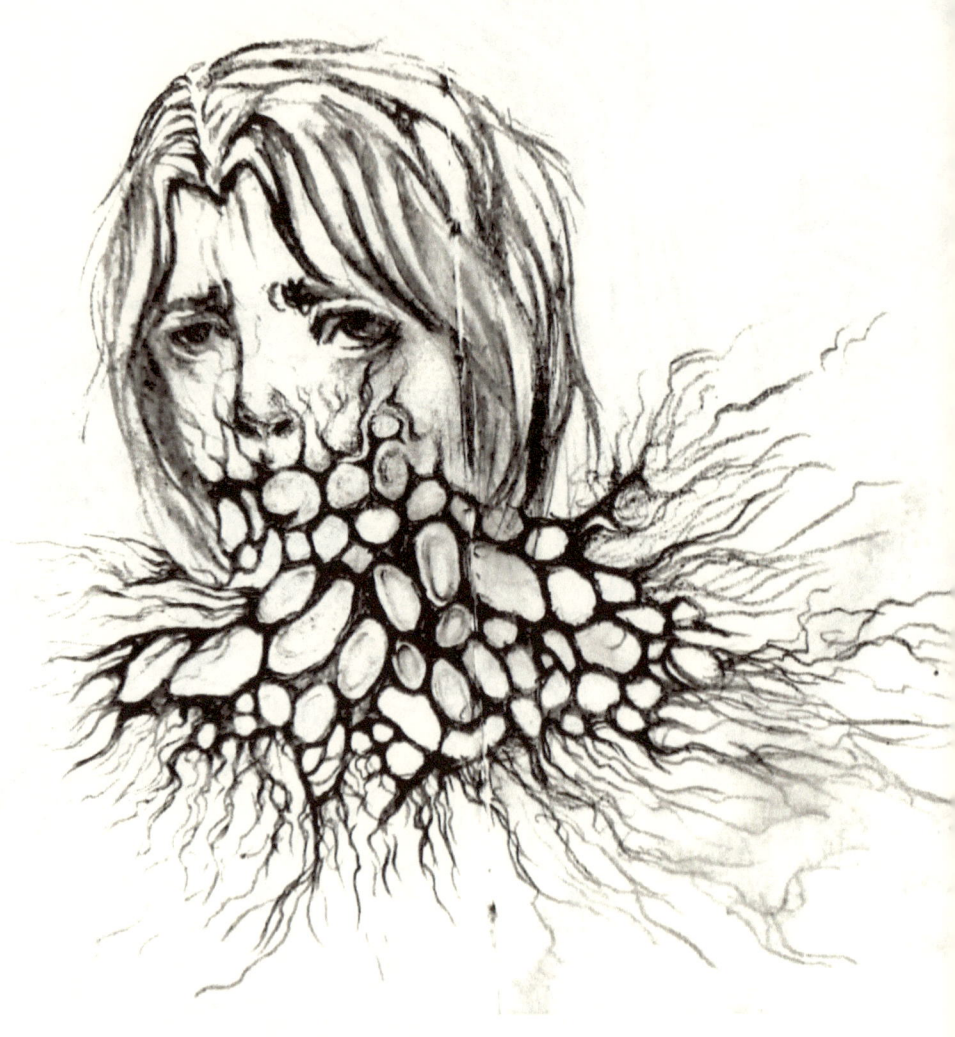

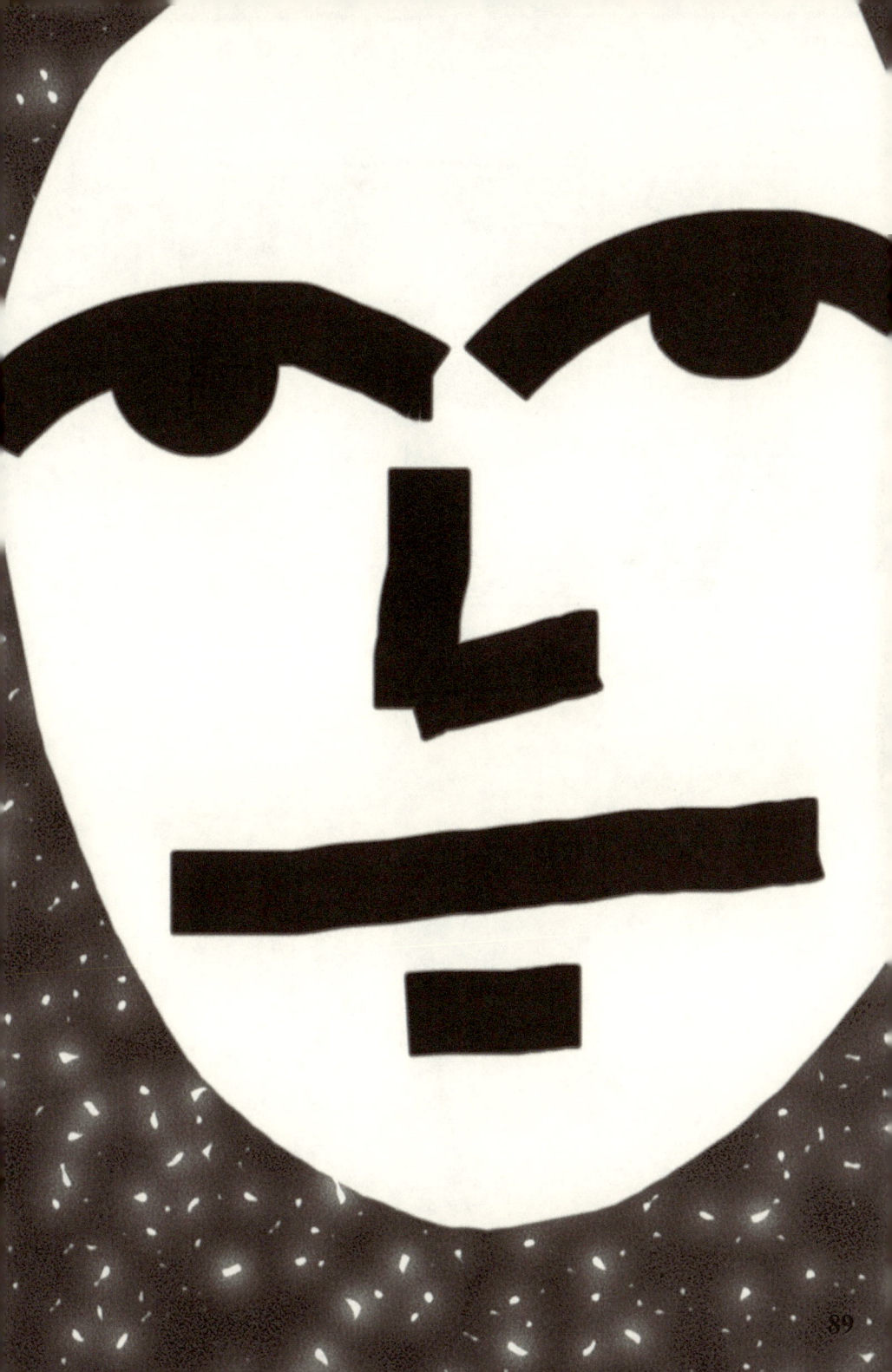

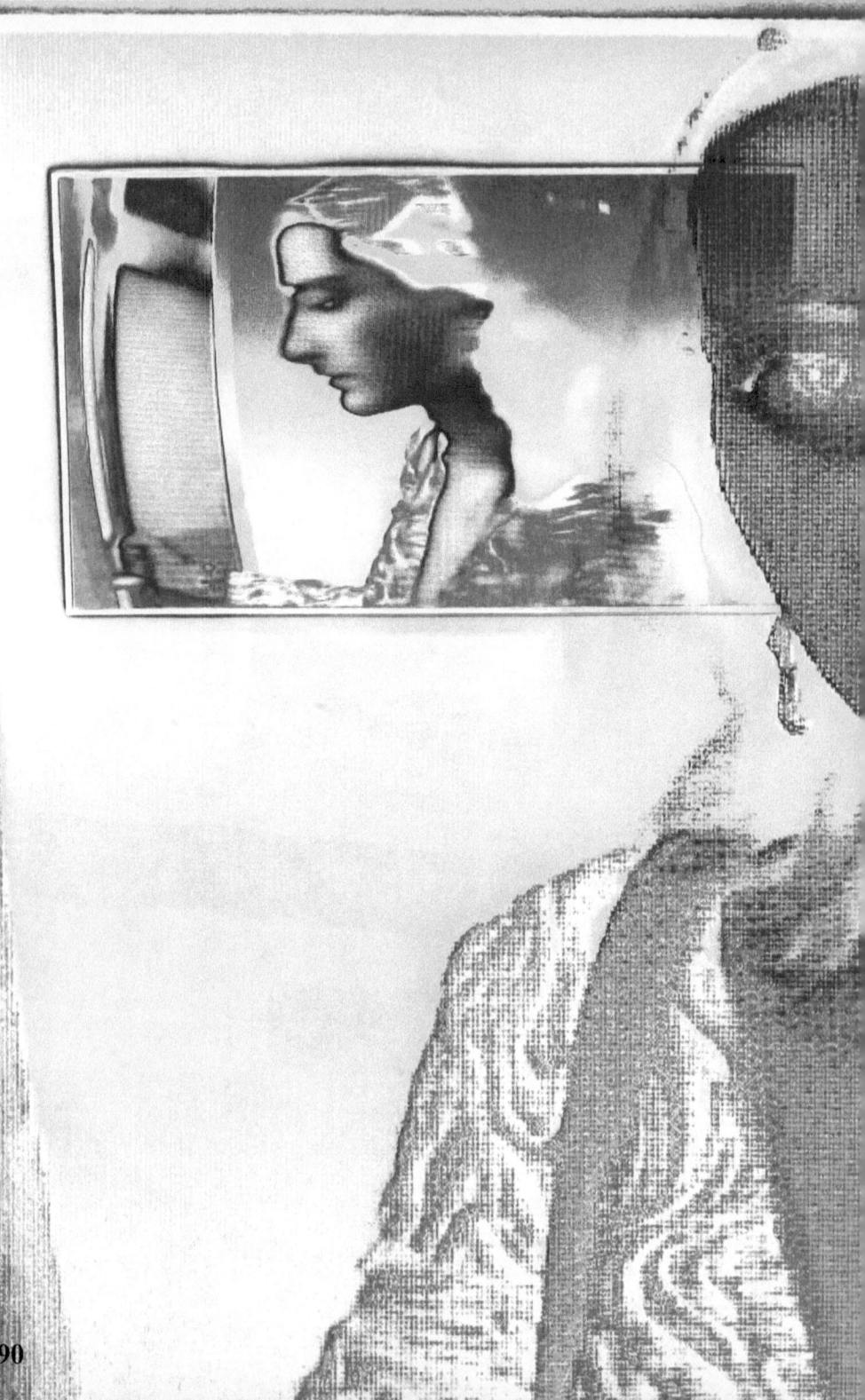

―ティストを育てるクリエイティブ工場
Creative factory nurtures young artists

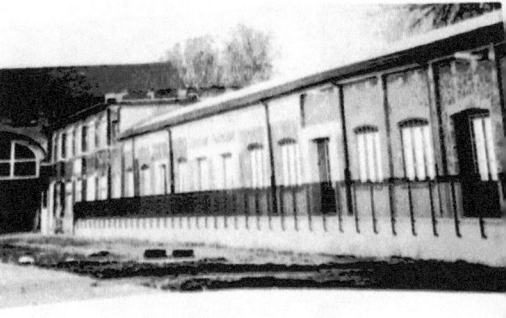

ミラノ市主宰の「ラ・ファブリカ・デル・
ヴァポーレ(蒸気工場)」が、2001年2月末に
オープンした。ここはアート、デザイン、写
真、音楽、演劇、ダンス、映画、文学などの文化
育成を目的としたオープン空間で、若者を
衆に開放される。

名前の由来は、ミラノ北西に位置する、か
蒸気機関車を製造していた工場跡地

Milan City's La Fabbrica del Vapore (The Ste
Factory) opened in late February 2001. The sp
is dedicated to nurturing such culture as art,
sign, music and theater, and was opened with
in mind.

name comes from the fact it occu
of a former factory that produced s
es. The building that forms the
space including the theater is scheduled for
vation, the plans and symbol for which were
lected in a competition between creators 35 y
under.

なっている現在
により両者が
アイデアの源
させたところなど
方向性を感じさせるエ
(文/中島恭子) ●

and Town Councilor for Y
says that "Nurturing cu
for local government g
between industry and
the space to serve as a br
culture, and guide to
the various problems

Held at the Ta
29, Century
tween 20th
cities, includ
New York.

In the London ex
and the works of de
among display
works extend
Chalayan's fu
everyone's e
McQueen and

In an age whe
designer and artist in separa
hibition gave visitors a glimpse of
in curation by displaying the wor
ers and artists in a limited tim
them to coexist without
and by inspiring visitors to

just the kind of projec
ting for. We can look for
community level a
xt by Hiromi Kim) ●

adelvapore.org

造力に期待したい。(文/ヒ.

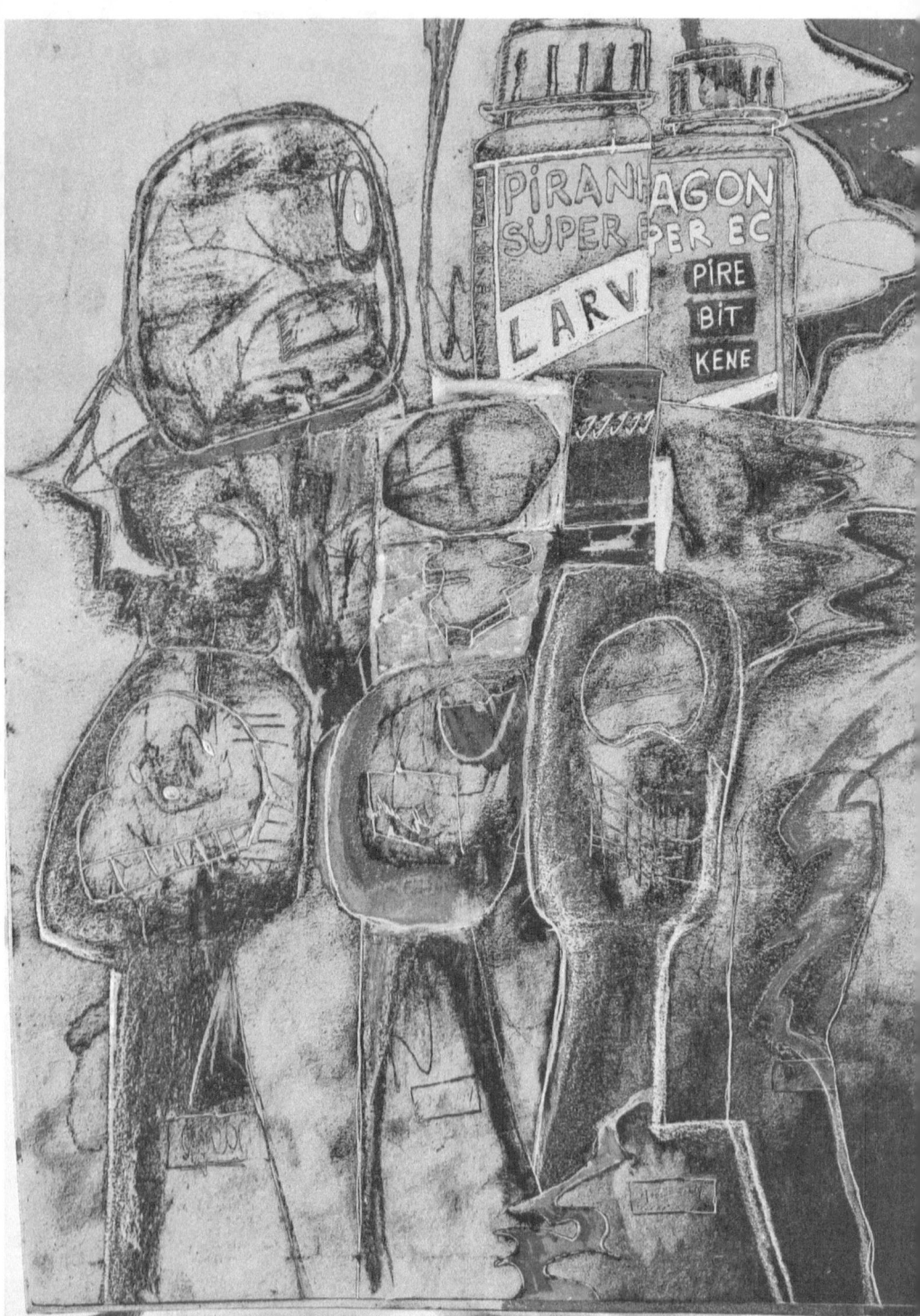

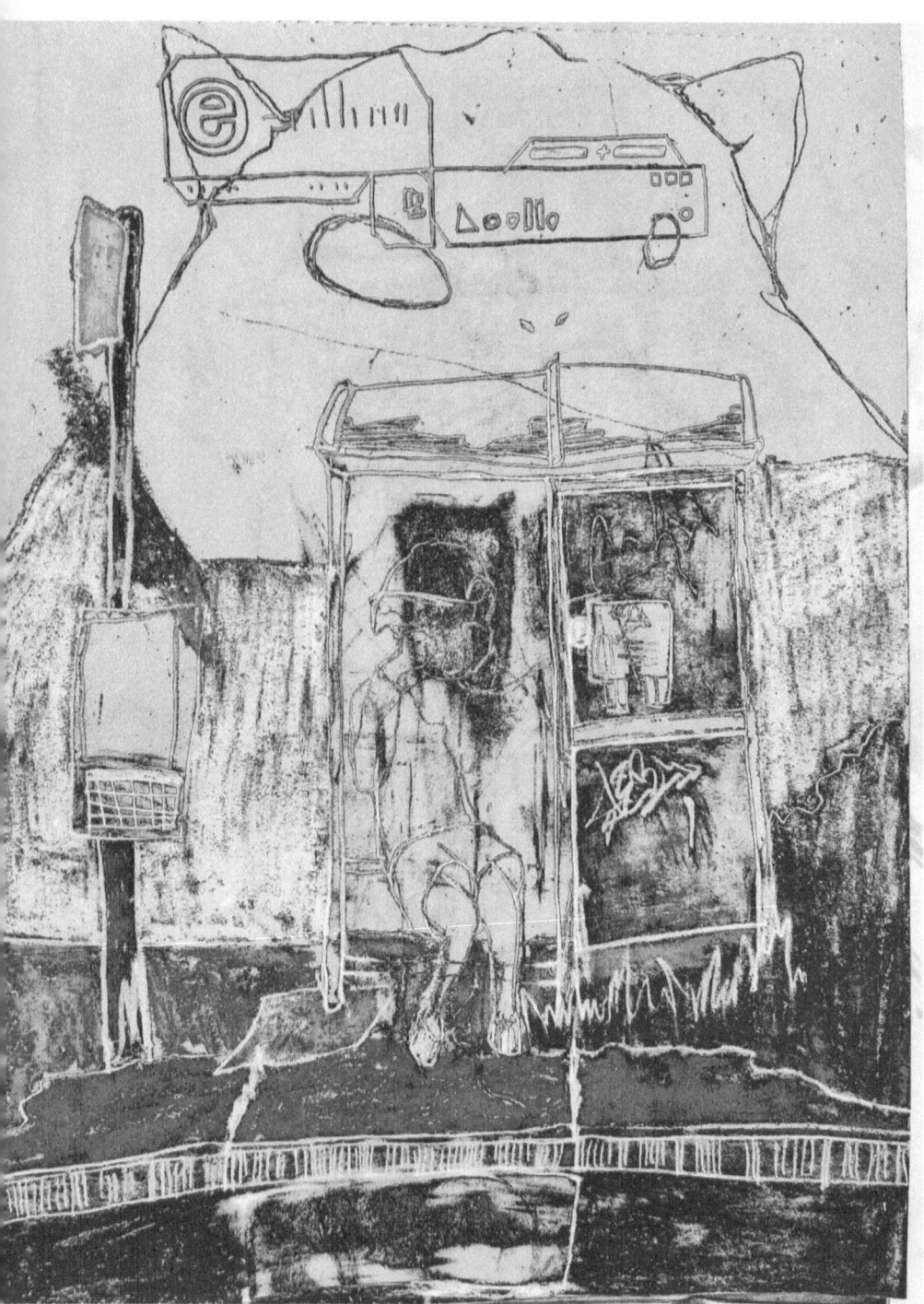

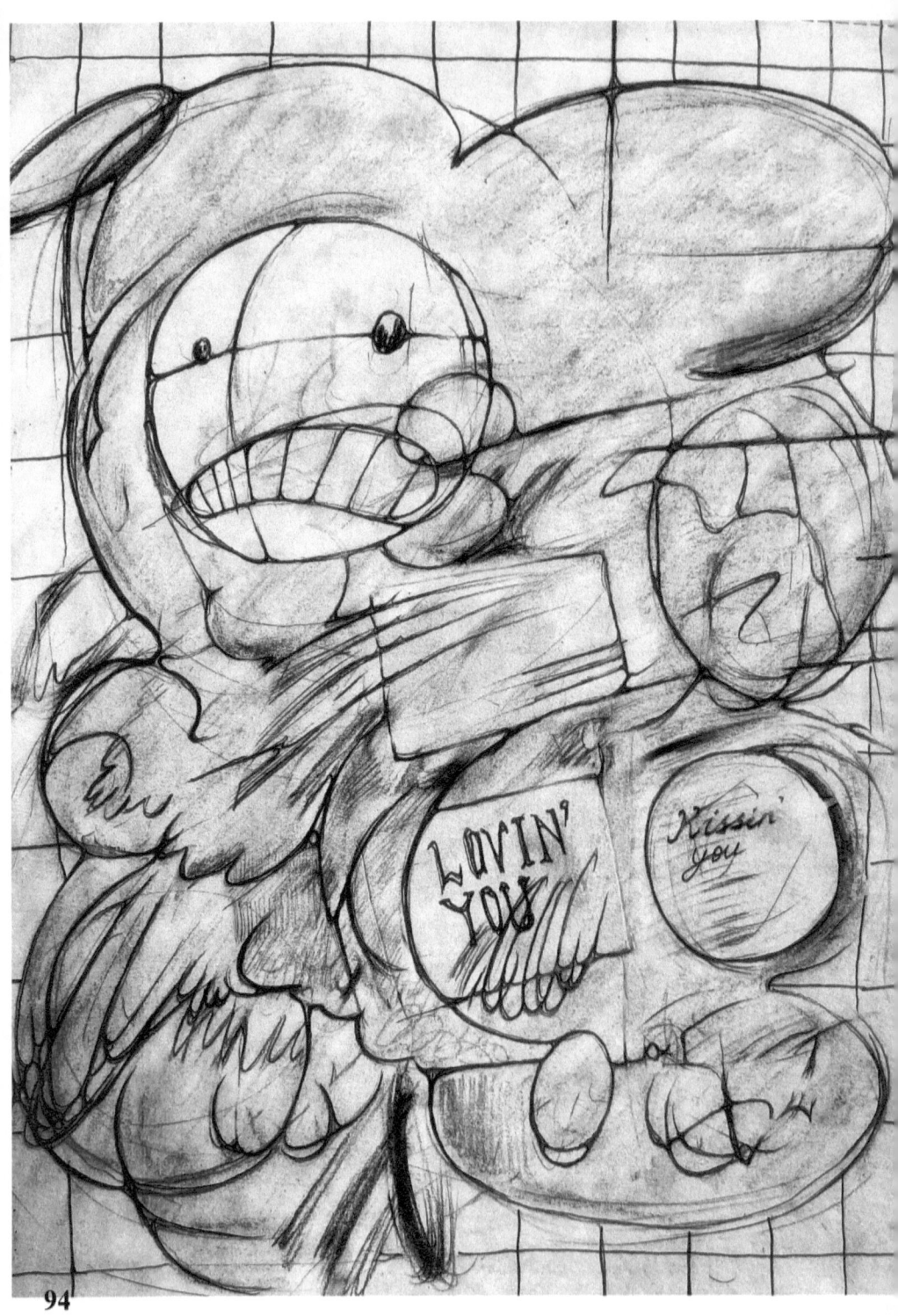

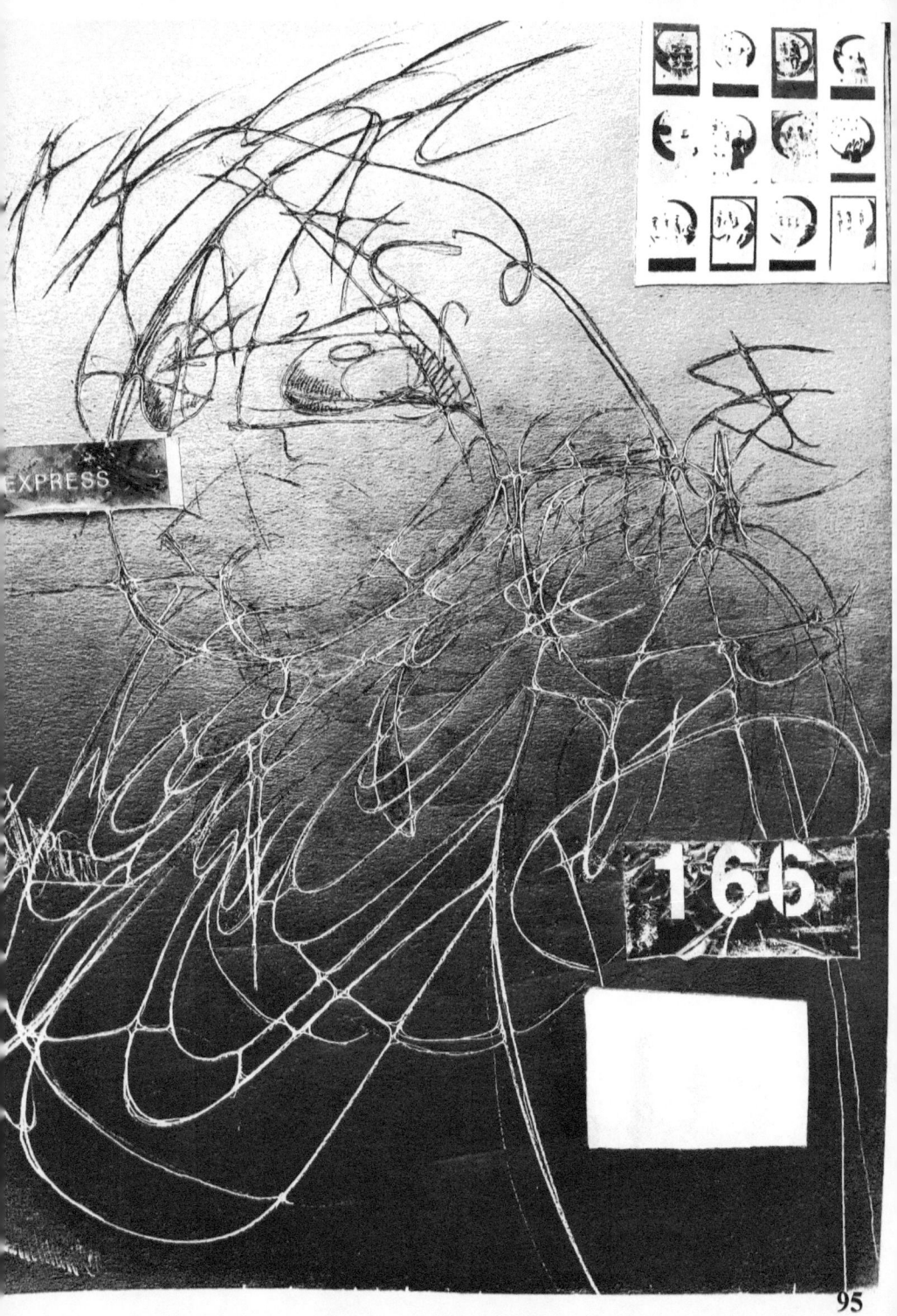

EXPRESS

166

أحبك

أنت جميلة

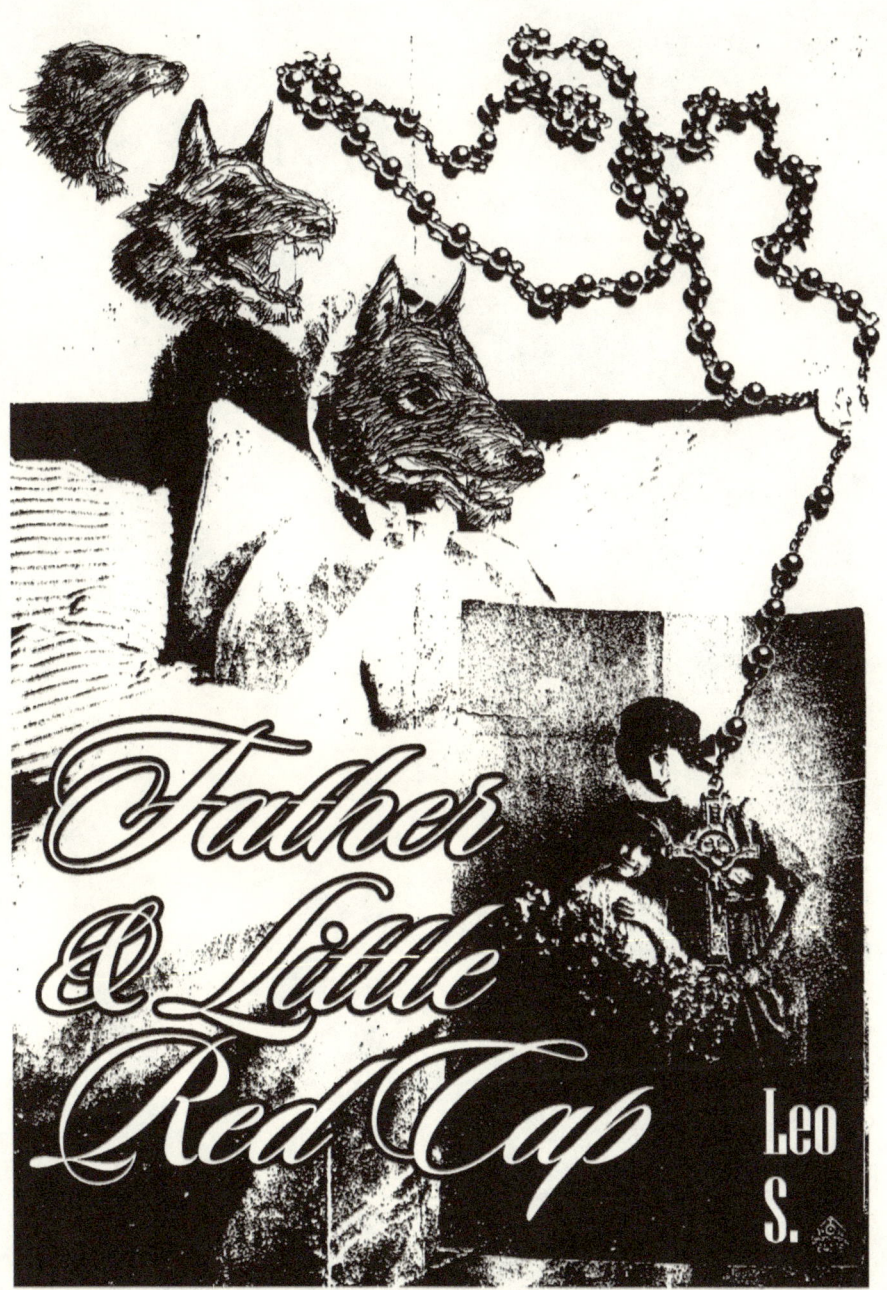

Father & Little Red Cap

Leo S.

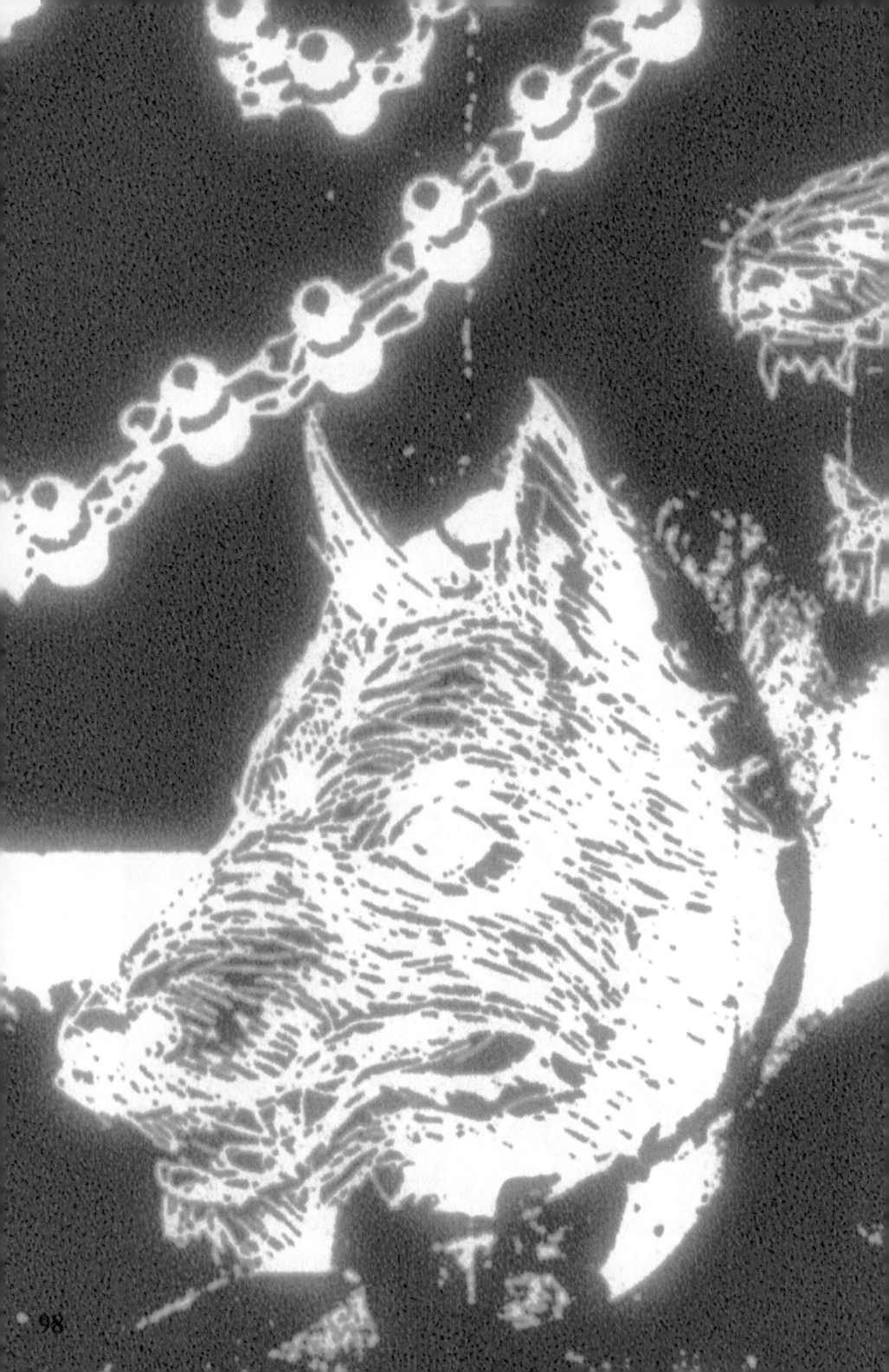

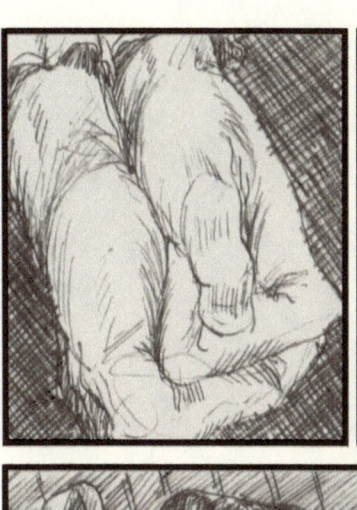
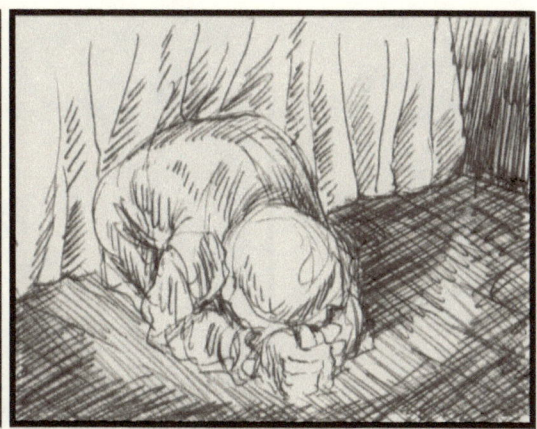
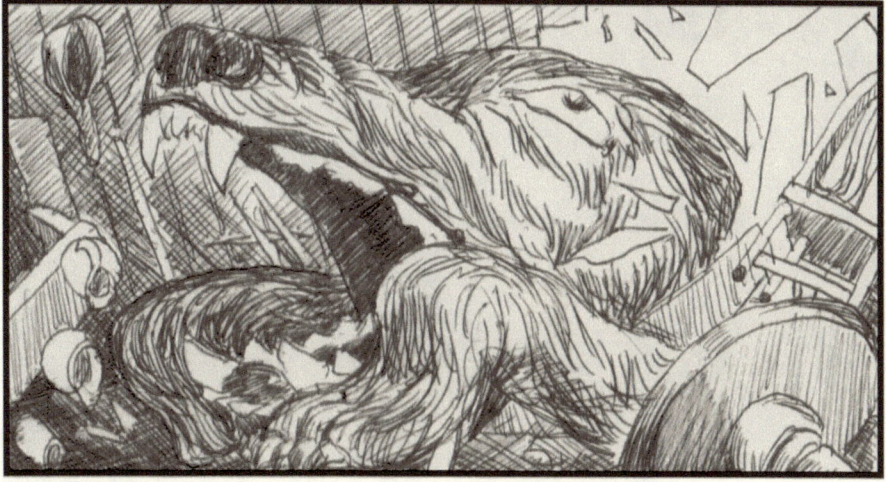
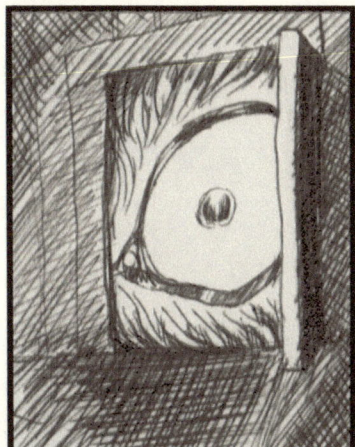
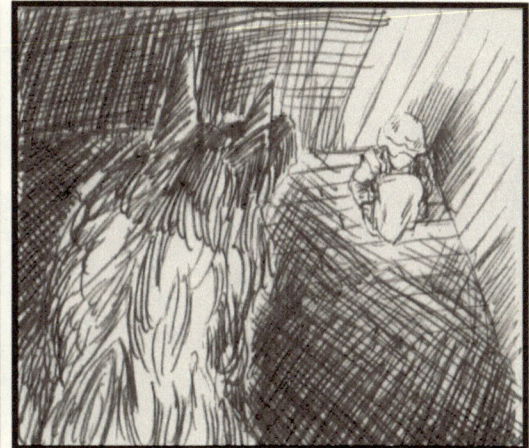

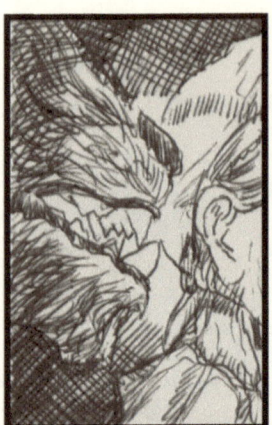
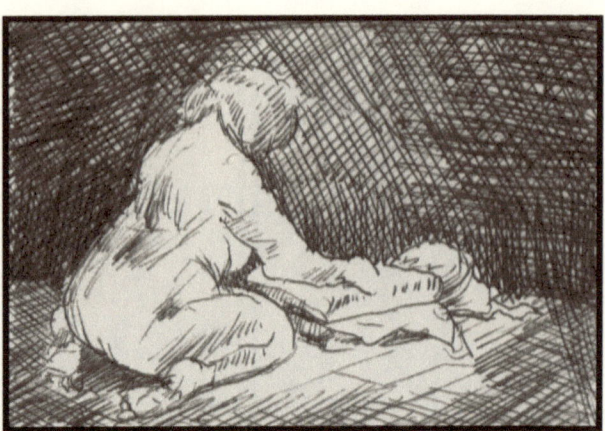
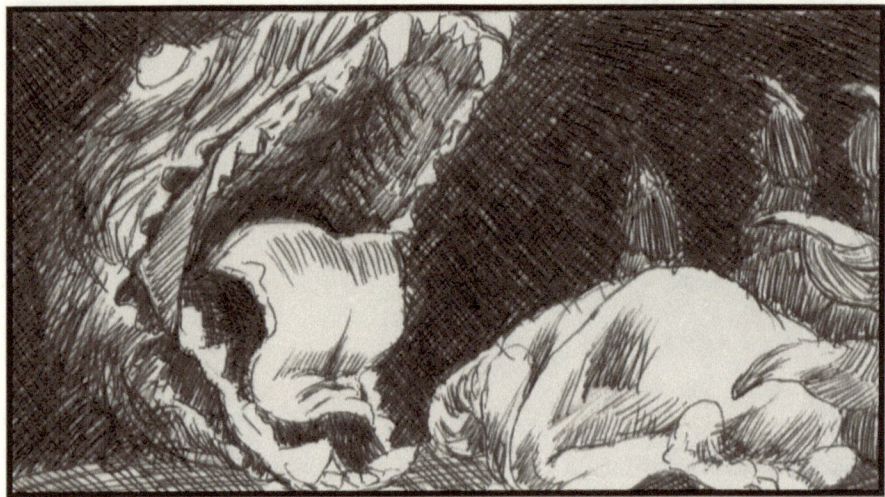
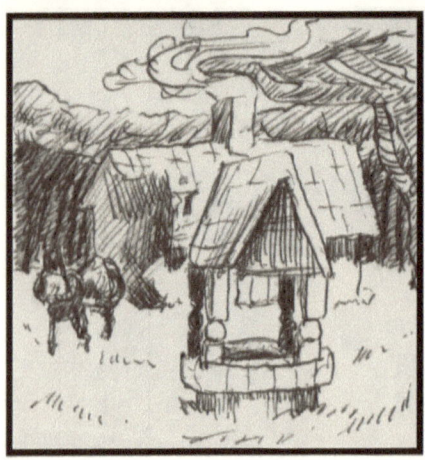
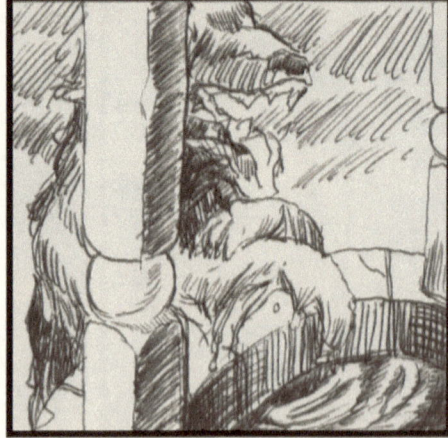

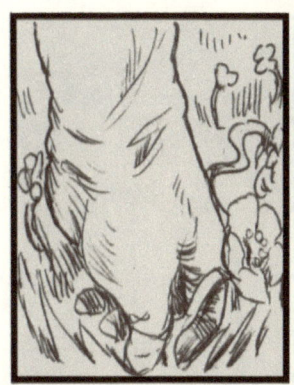
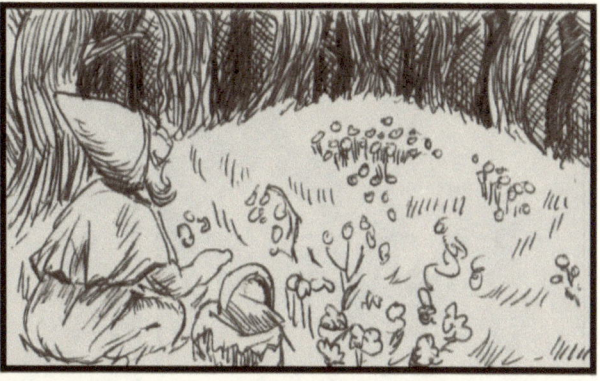
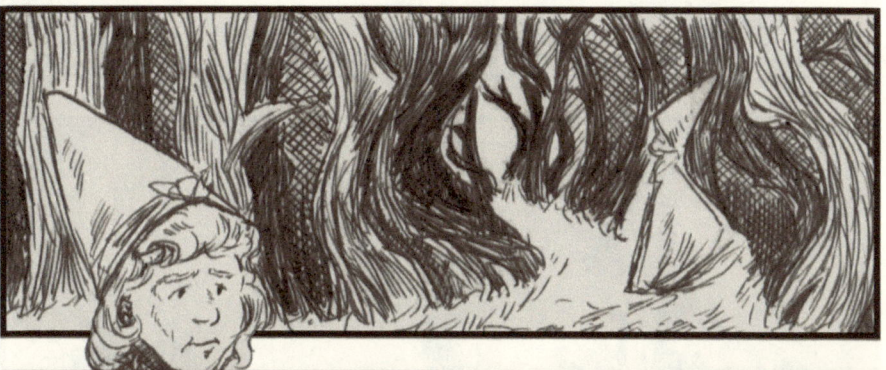
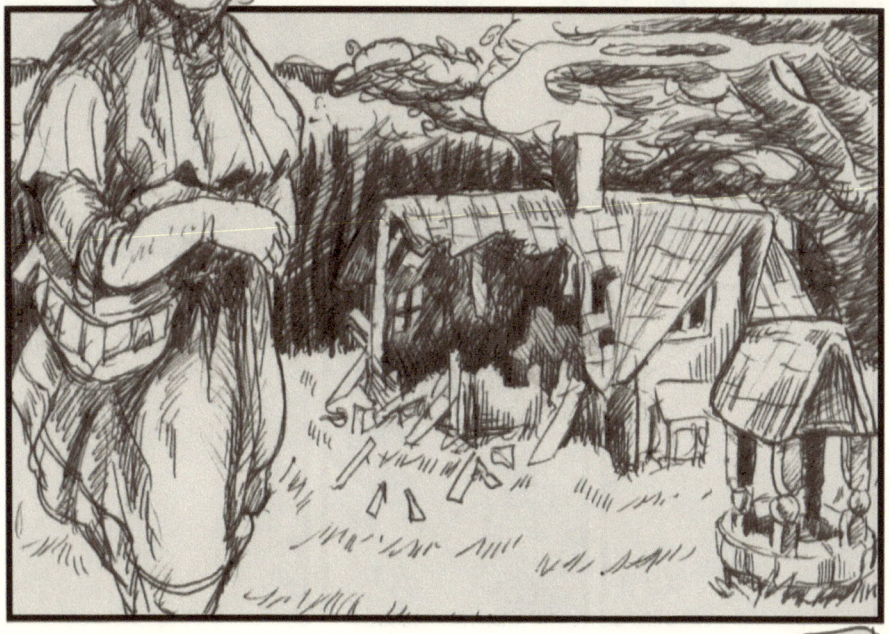

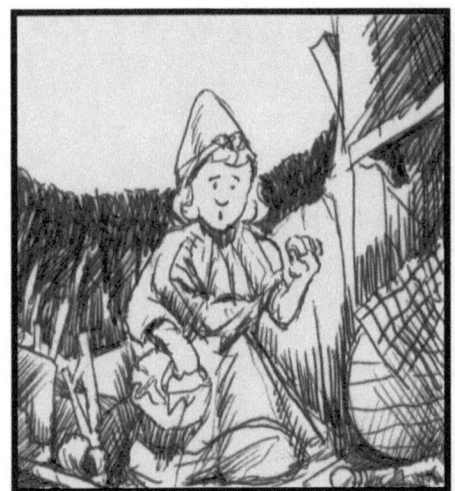
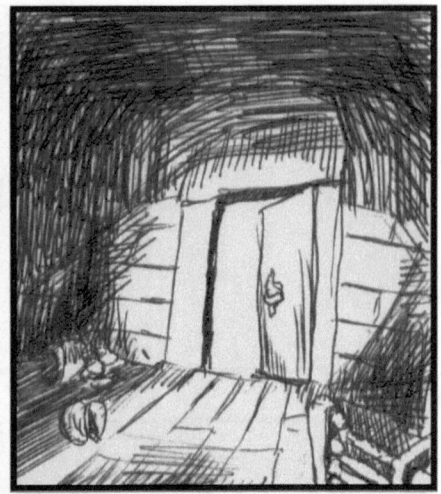
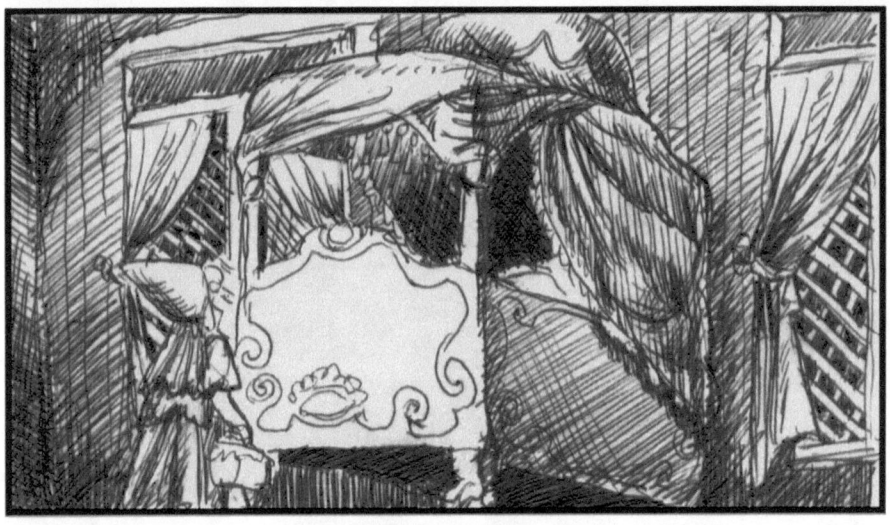
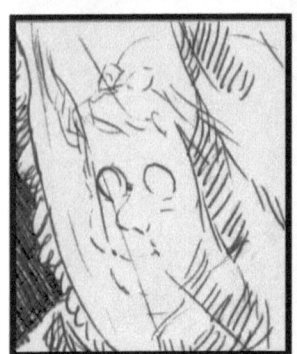
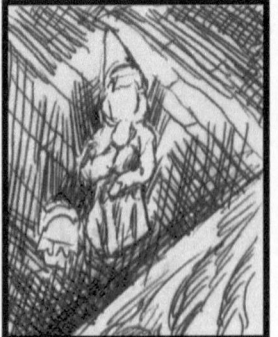
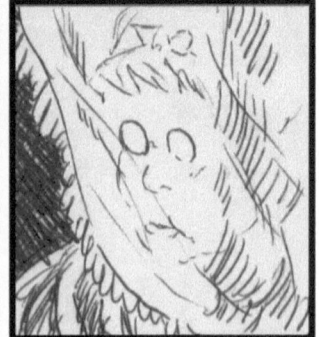

L,S

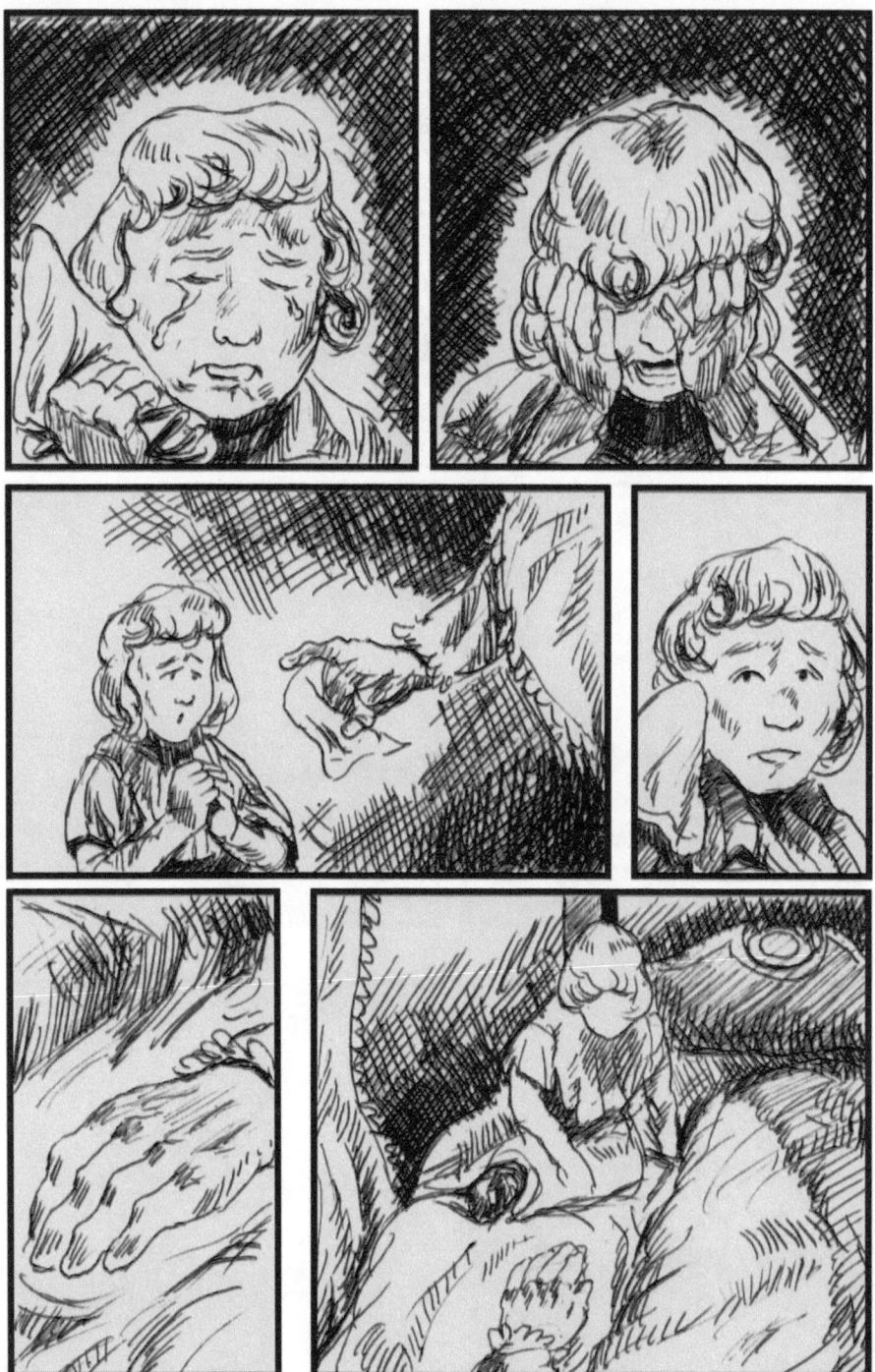

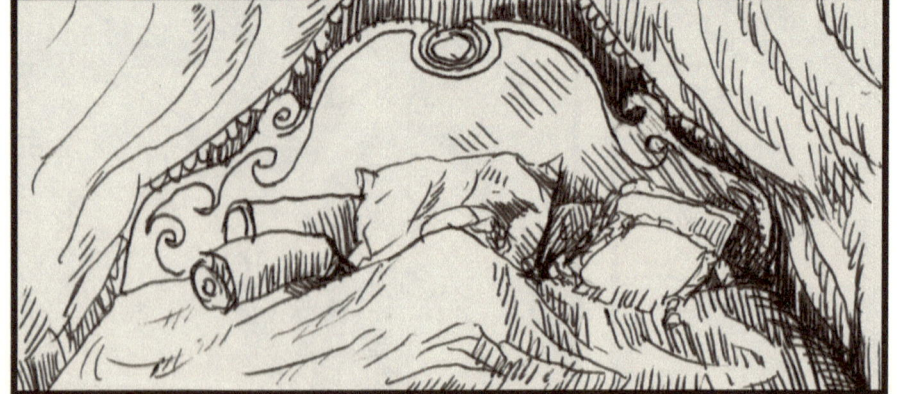

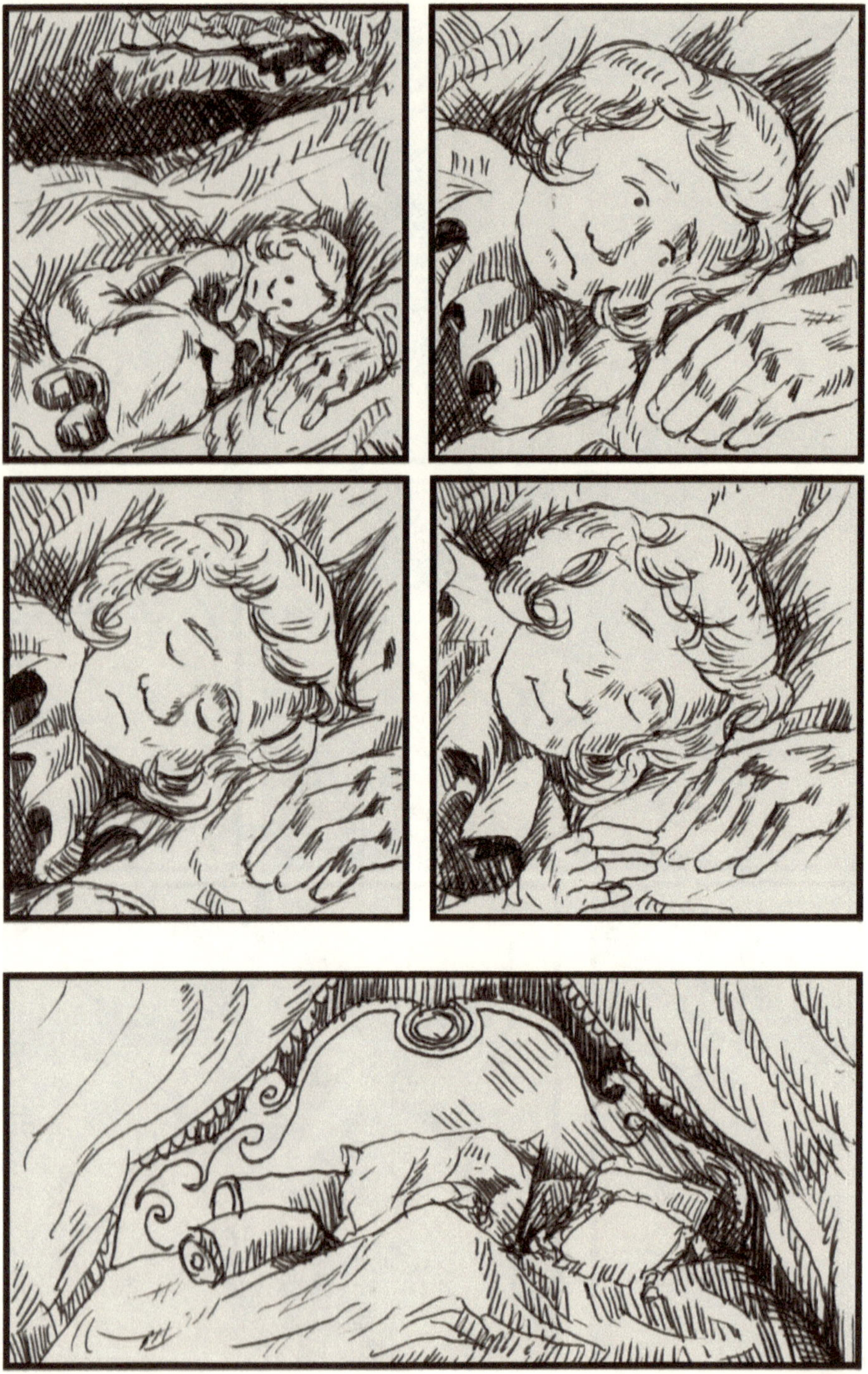

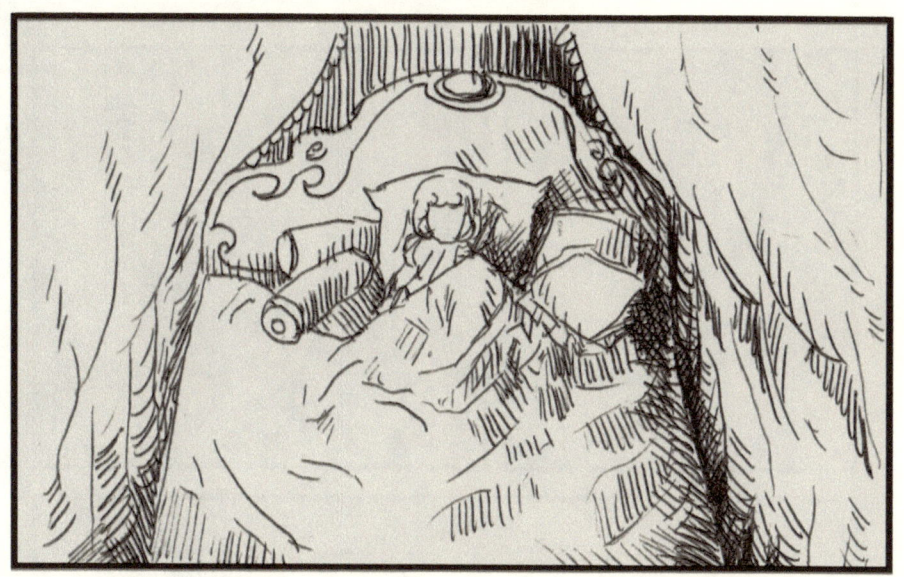

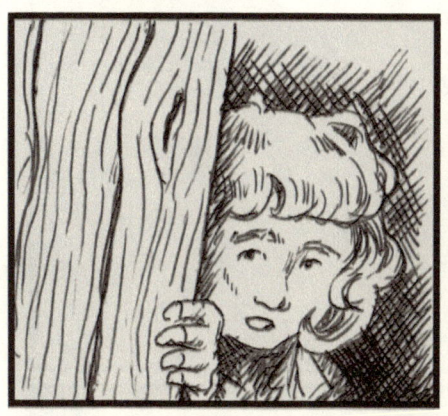

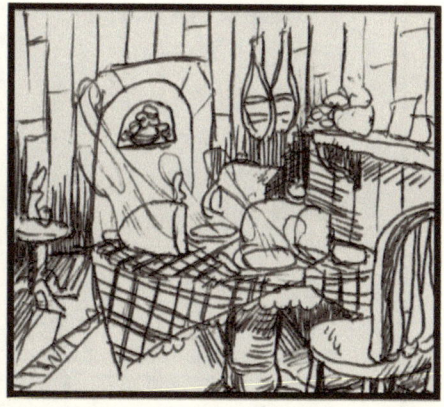

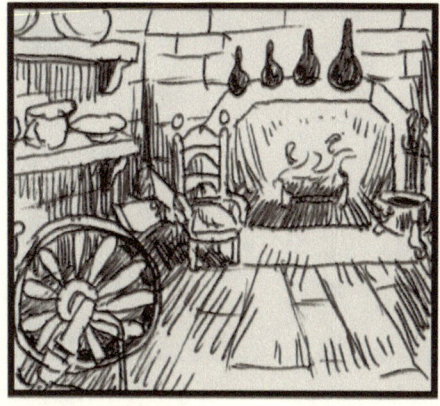

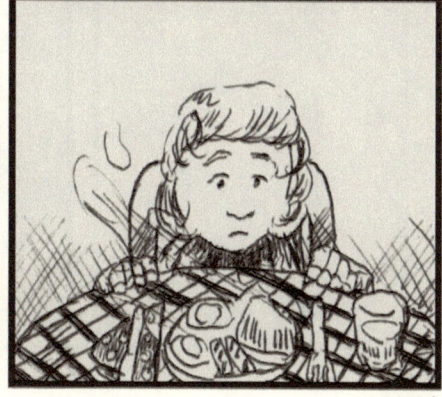

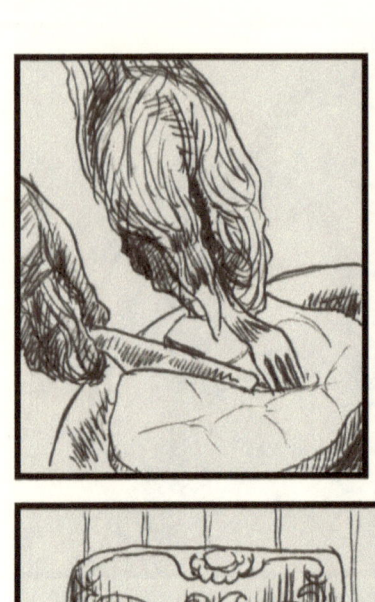
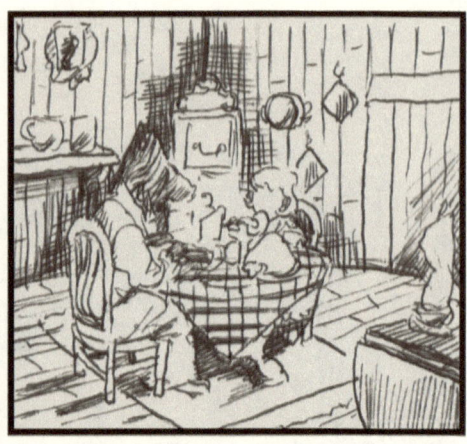
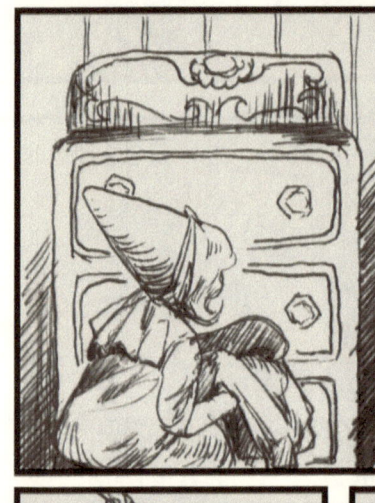
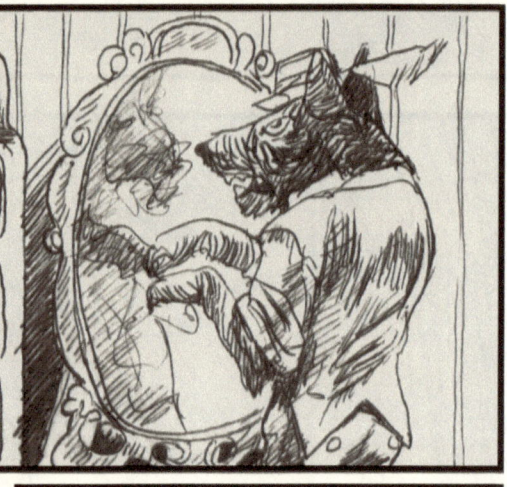
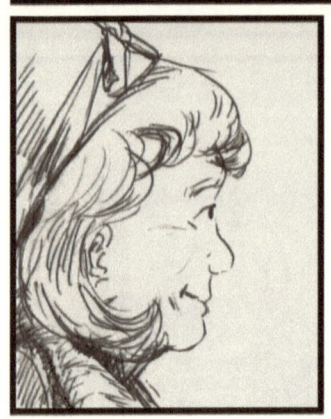
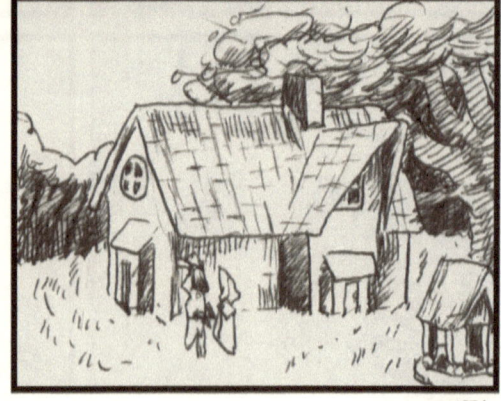

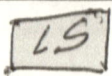

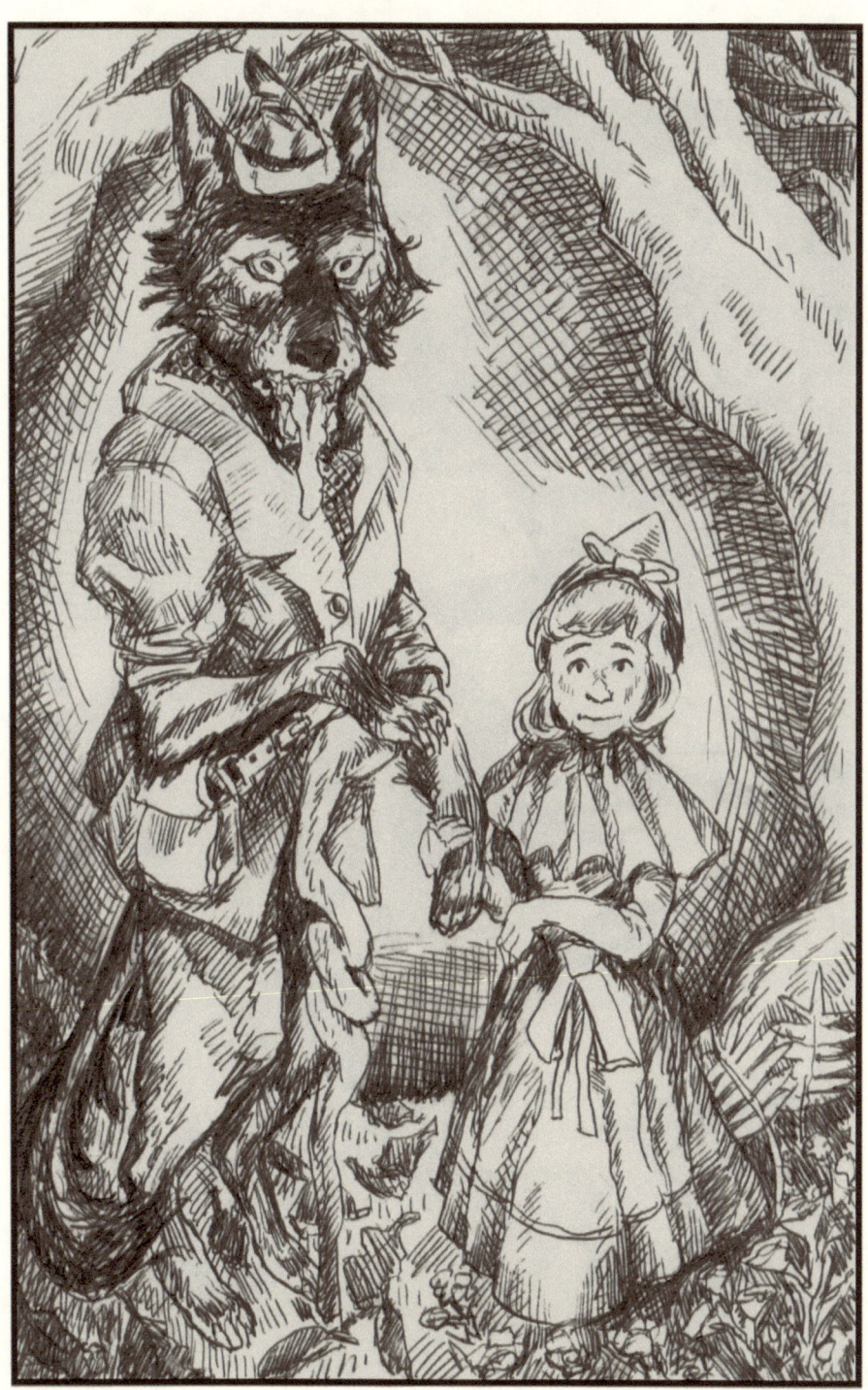

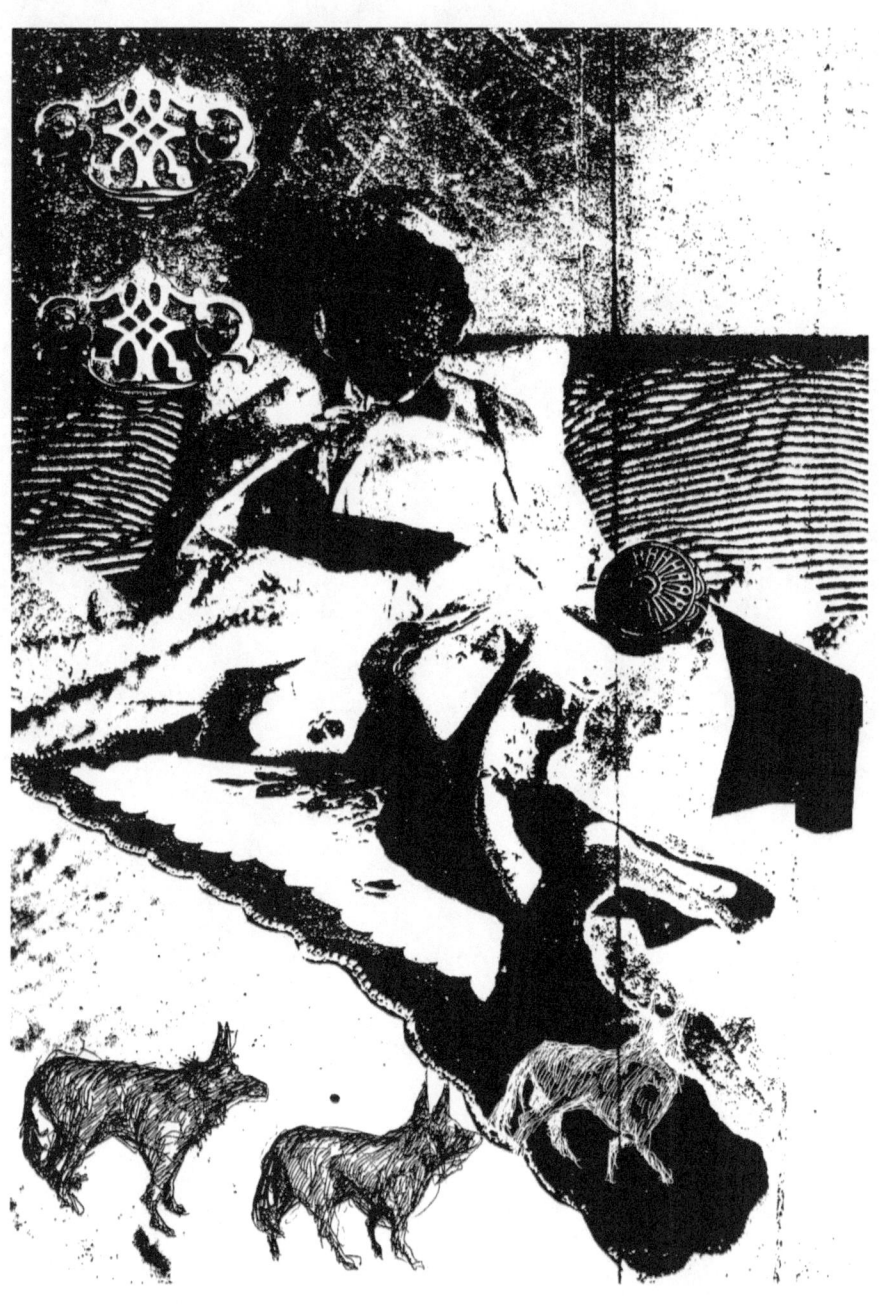

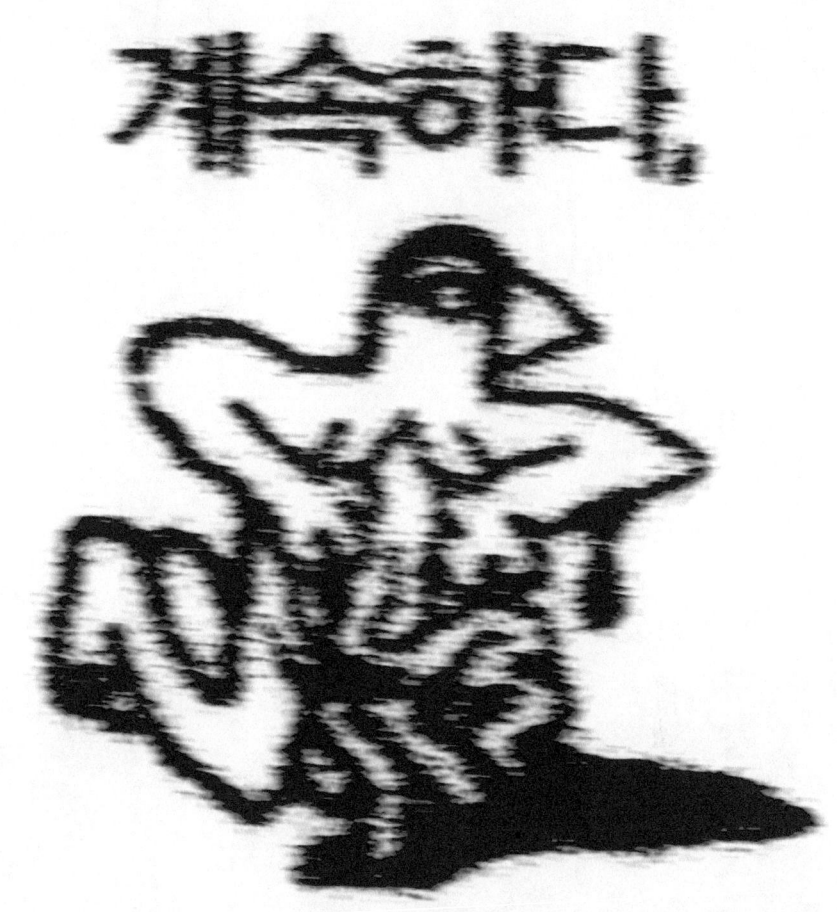

계속한다.

당신은 반전의
지지해야한다

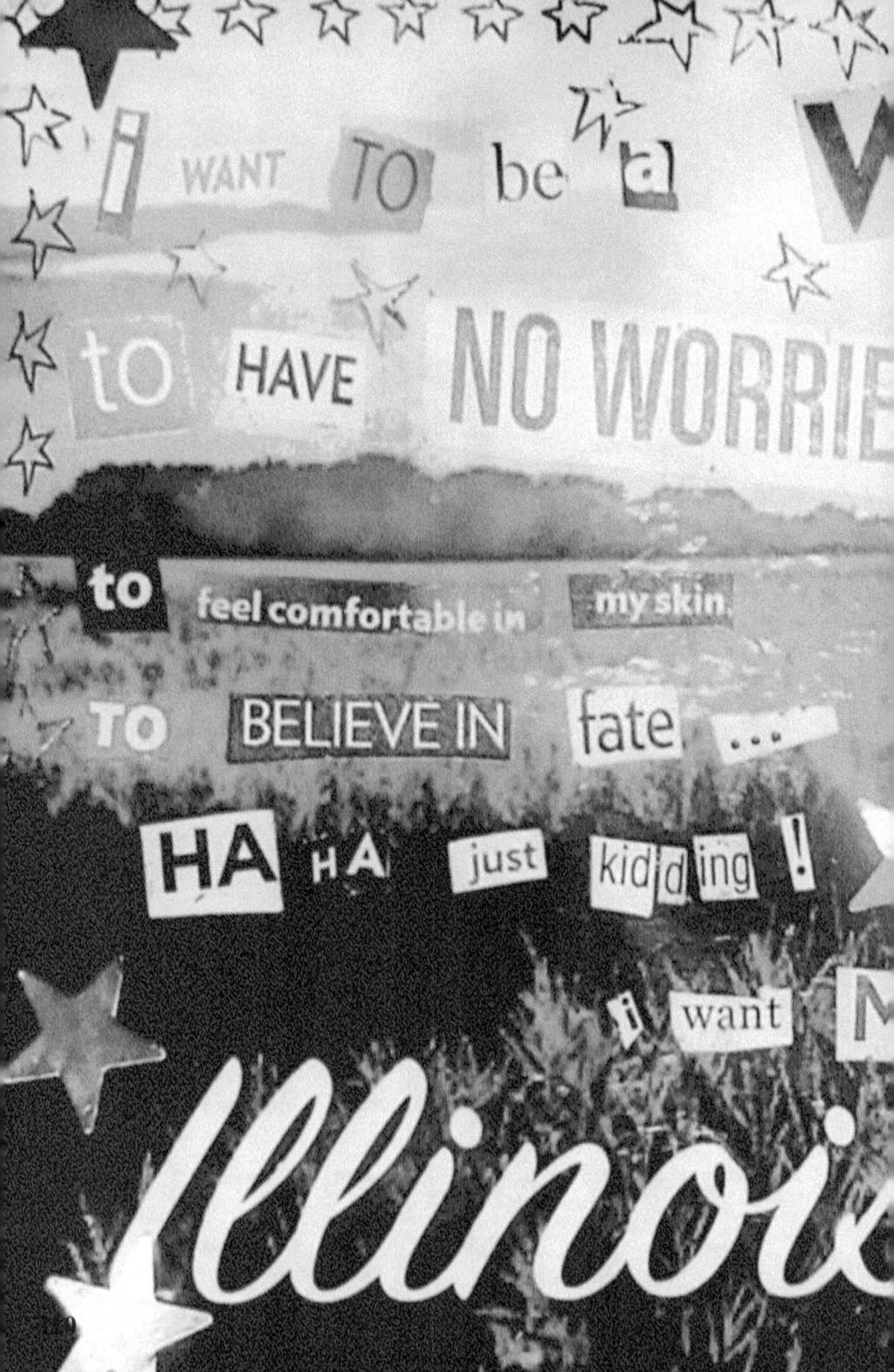

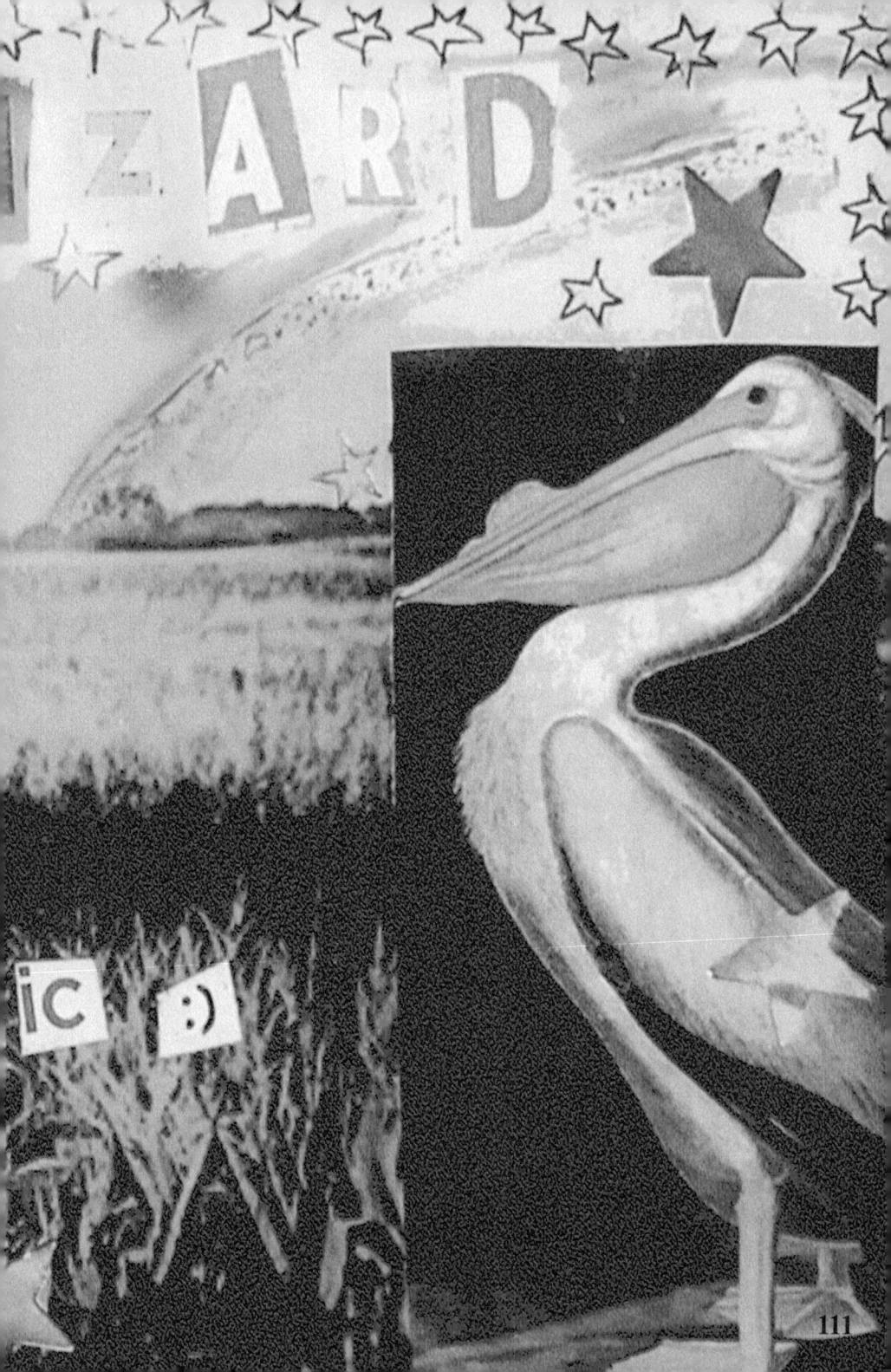

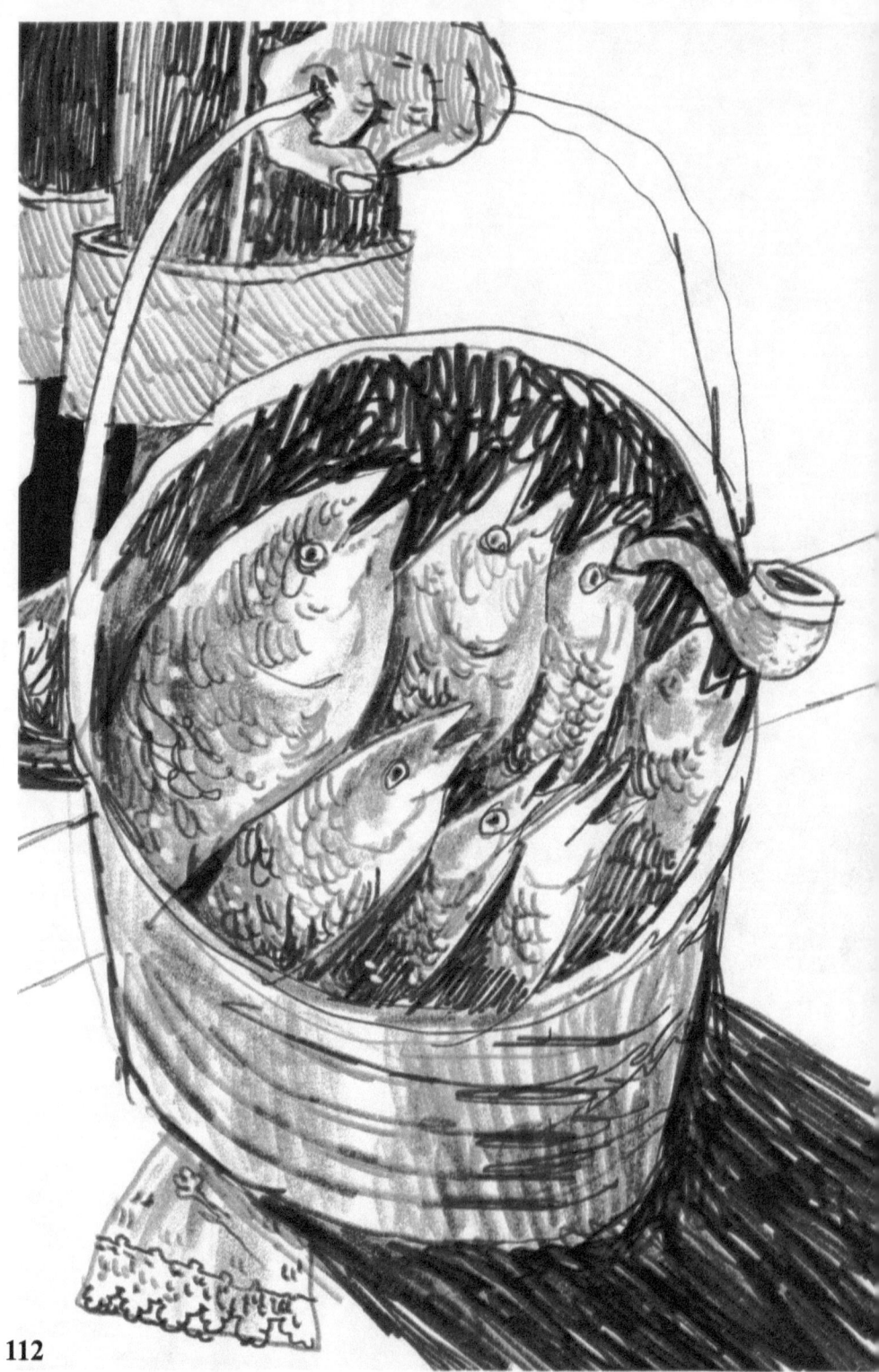

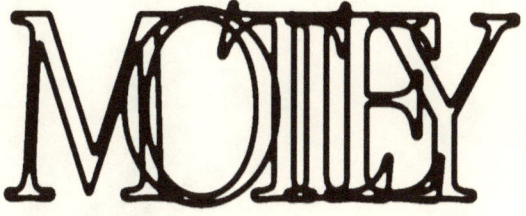

MOTLEY MAG
WILL HAVE A
FOURTH
ISSUE

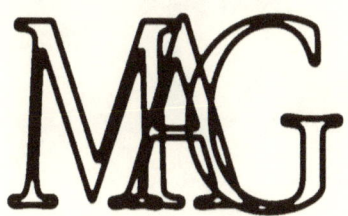

www.ingramcontent.com/pod-product-compliance
Lightning Source LLC
Chambersburg PA
CBHW021832170526
45157CB00007B/2782